RAMEN
TO THE RESCUE COOKBOOK

RAMEN
TO THE RESCUE COOKBOOK

Over **100** Creative Recipes for Easy Meals
Using Everyone's Favorite Pack of Noodles

Jessica Harlan

Ulysses Press

Published by:
ULYSSES PRESS
P.O. Box 3440
Berkeley, CA 94703
www.ulyssespress.com

ISBN: 978-1-56975-990-5
Library of Congress Catalog Number 2011926033

Printed in the United States by Bang Printing

10 9 8 7 6 5 4 3 2

Acquisitions editor: Keith Riegert
Managing editor: Claire Chun
Editors: Lauren Harrison, Leslie Evans
Proofreader: Elyce Berrigan-Dunlop
Production: Judith Metzener
Illustrations: Evan Wondolowski
Cover photograph: shrimp and noodle dish © High Impact Photography/
    istockphoto.com; ramen noodles © yellowsarah/istockphoto.com
Design: what!design @ whatweb.com

Distributed by Publishers Group West

To Chip, the sous chef in my kitchen and in my life,

and

to Sadie and Gillian, the best taste testers a cook could ever hope for.

TABLE OF CONTENTS

ACKNOWLEDGMENTS

I am grateful to everyone who came along for the ride on this wonderful adventure of writing my first cookbook—particularly the team at Ulysses Press, who gave me this opportunity and were so pleasant to work with.

A hug to all of my friends in Atlanta, New York, Chicago, and elsewhere who chimed in with ideas, recipes, and encouragement. And a special shout-out to my virtual office mate Stacie McClintock, who sent me the e-mail that got this whole ball rolling.

A raise of the glass to my good friend Kelley Sparwasser, who let me tap into her endless font of fantastic ideas, and who helped me out with several recipes. And to her husband, Adam Wisniewski, for his wonderful Ramen Mary recipe.

Love to my parents-in-law, Joseph and Christina Harlan, who let me use their kitchen, their babysitting services, and their taste buds on countless occasions. And I am eternally grateful to my brother-in-law Steve Harlan, who's always got my back when it comes to legal matters.

And more love to my own parents, Judy and Greg Goldbogen, my most faithful supporters throughout my life, enthusiastically endorsing my decisions and ideas, and championing every accomplishment.

And finally, much love and gratitude to my family. To my husband, Chip Harlan, who is infinitely supportive and proud of me, who eagerly sampled every dish I set before him without ever uttering the words, "Ramen, again?" And to my daughters, Sadie and Gillian, who are thankfully the least picky eaters I know, and the best daughters I could possibly have wished for.

INTRODUCTION

The mere mention of ramen noodles is sure to elicit nostalgia. Many people have memories of living on those little packages of noodles and powdered soup seasoning when they were in college or as they tried to make ends meet on an entry-level paycheck.

And indeed, for the budget conscious, packaged ramen noodles are the perfect food: They're cheap (my local supermarket sells six for $1), fast (the noodles cook in 3 minutes), and filling.

Admittedly, ramen soup, with its salty broth and freeze-dried vegetables, can get a little boring after a while. And certainly the sodium-laden seasoning packet isn't really that great for you . . . but that's where this book comes in. You can take advantage of the convenience, low price, and speedy cooking time of instant ramen noodles but use your own fresh ingredients, sauces, and seasonings to create a multitude of different dishes. Veggie-laden stir fries, delicious soups, innovative appetizers, crisp salads, casseroles big enough to feed a crowd—all these and more can be made with those cheap little packages of ramen noodles.

And because the long curly noodles are part of our collective culinary experience, a dish made with ramen noodles—especially when they're used in an unconventional way—is sure to be quite a conversation starter.

So stock up on those little packages, because with *Ramen to the Rescue* in your hands, you're sure to find many more delicious uses for instant ramen noodles than you ever dreamed you would!

Ramen: A Brief Background

Although ramen noodles are typically thought of as a Japanese food, they actually have China to credit for their origin. After all, noodles and pasta originated in China thousands of years ago. According to one theory, in the early 1900s, Chinese cooks in a Tokyo restaurant created a brothy noodle soup called *shina soba*. Soba is a type of Asian noodle made with buckwheat, rather than the wheat flour that ramen noodles are made of.

RAMEN SOUP MINI RECIPES: 10 EASY WAYS TO JAZZ UP RAMEN

When you just feel like keeping it simple but still want to add some dimension to a bowl of ramen noodle soup, use one of these mini recipes to add just one or two ingredients to your dish.

1. Stir a handful of chopped scallions into the soup just before serving.

2. Sprinkle the soup with fresh cilantro or Thai basil leaves just before serving.

3. Stir in a squirt of Sriracha or other Asian hot sauce along with the ramen noodle seasoning packet.

4. Add about ½ teaspoon toasted sesame oil to the broth and sprinkle with toasted sesame seeds.

5. Stir in a handful of chopped firm tofu or cooked chicken before serving.

6. Add about ½ cup frozen edamame or frozen chopped spinach to the boiling water along with the noodles.

7. After adding the seasoning packet to the cooked noodles and broth, stir in 1 lightly beaten egg until the egg cooks, and add a dash of soy sauce. Or, top with a chopped hard-boiled egg, or a fried or poached egg.

8. Garnish the soup with a handful of mung beans or shredded cabbage and a squeeze of lime.

9. Sprinkle the soup with *nori furikake* (seaweed seasoning), to taste.

10. As the noodles cook, add sliced cremini mushrooms or reconstituted dried mushrooms, such as shiitake or oyster mushrooms, to the pan.

Shina soba became Japan's most popular Chinese dish and was served all over the country, with different regions incorporating local ingredients to make the recipe their own. Later, the name "ramen" was coined; it's the Japanese pronunciation of "lo mein," the Chinese noodles.

In 1958, Momofuku Ando of Nissin Foods developed a chicken-flavored instant ramen noodle product in an effort to provide an easy-to-produce, convenient food option for citizens in postwar Japan, where food was scarce and finances were strained. At first, Ando's ramen was considered a luxury, since it was still more expensive for consumers than fresh Japanese udon noodles. But eventually people grew to appreciate the convenience, and soon other manufacturers of instant ramen noodles came on board with their own versions and flavors.

In the early 1970s, Ando developed another ramen innovation: packing the noodles in a polystyrene cup so they could cook in boiling water right in the package. The concept of instant ramen noodles spread worldwide, and several manufacturers opened factories in the United States, an ideal marketplace for a product of this kind, since Americans have such a need and appreciation for cheap, convenient food. Nissin's ramen, sold under the names Top Ramen and Cup Noodles, is today one of the best-selling ramen brands in

> In Thailand, sales of instant ramen noodles have been used as an economic indicator, dubbed the Mama Noodles Index. Skyrocketing sales of the country's best-selling instant ramen brand, Mama Noodles, accurately predicted a weakening economy.

America, along with Maruchan, a brand started in California in 1977.

True ramen fans can visit the Momofuku Ando Instant Ramen Museum in Osaka, Japan. The museum includes a reproduction of the "research shack" where Ando perfected his recipe, as well as an exhibit of production methods, a display of ramen noodle products from around the world, a video of the manufacturing process, and a tasting room. There's also a hands-on workshop where you can try making your own instant ramen noodles, from stirring up the noodle dough to drying the noodles in the flash-fryer, and another interactive exhibit where you can make your own instant noodle cup.

How Instant Ramen Is Made

Have you ever wondered how those little rectangular bricks of dry noodles are produced? A look at the manufacturing process is fascinating indeed, which might explain why the Maruchan factory was once featured on an episode of the Food Network show *Unwrapped*, and the ramen manufacturer Nongshim hosts official factory tours.

Maruchan Ramen was the official soup of the 1984 Summer Olympics in Los Angeles.

At the beginning of the process, ramen is made similarly to any other noodle or pasta: Flour, water, and other ingredients are mixed and kneaded in giant mixers, and then the dough is stretched into a thin sheet between two enormous rollers.

As the dough is cut into thin noodle strands, it becomes curly because of the slow speed at which the noodles exit the cutters. The curly noodles, in 100-foot lengths, travel on a moving bed through a hot steam chamber where they cook for 1 minute. The steam-cooked noodles are cut into portions called pillows, then dipped into a deep-fryer where they cook briefly at 400°F. When the fryer finishes the cooking process, it removes the moisture from the noodles so they're dry and shelf-stable. Then the noodle pillows are paired with a seasoning packet and packaged in their plastic wrapper.

Your Ramen to the Rescue Pantry

There are a number of pantry staples that you'll find yourself reaching for again and again to make these recipes. Here's a little explanation about some of the ingredients you'll find in this book.

Coconut Milk: Rich canned coconut milk is delicious in sweet and savory recipes. It comes in regular and light versions; as you can imagine, the regular version, which contains much more fat, has a creamier mouthfeel and a slightly deeper flavor. But you can substitute the light version if you are trying to be healthier.

Curry Paste: Jarred curry paste and a can of coconut milk is all you need to make Thai-style curries. Thai curry paste typically comes in red or green. One is not spicier than the other; instead, the red curry paste has a deeper, more roasted flavor, and the green curry paste has an earthier flavor. Try both to see which one you prefer.

Edamame: You can find frozen edamame (soy) beans in almost any supermarket these days. These nutty-tasting beans, which look like lima beans but have a firmer texture and a slightly sweeter flavor, are delicious additions to stir-fries, soups, salads, and other dishes. Choose the shelled variety to save yourself some work, and keep a bag on hand in the freezer.

Fish Sauce: This Thai condiment is made from fish (usually anchovies) that is fermented with salt and water. It is a clear, thin, salty liquid that is used to season soups and sauces. You can find vegetarian versions made from soy. The sauce will keep indefinitely in a cool, dry place. I prefer to keep mine in the refrigerator, although it isn't necessary.

Ginger: Many of the Asian-influenced recipes in this book, particularly those in the Asian-Inspired Classics chapter (page 109), rely on a hint of ginger to give them an authentic flavor. You can find fresh ginger root in the produce aisle at the grocery store. To use it, peel the brown skin with a paring knife or a vegetable peeler, then chop or finely grate the yellowish interior (a Microplane-type grater is

Instant ramen noodles are truly a part of American pop culture. A 2010 memoir, *The Ramen King and I* by journalist Andy Raskin, poses instant-ramen inventor Momofuku Ando as Raskin's idol whilst the author self-analyzes his failed love life. A 2008 film called *The Ramen Girl* stars Brittany Murphy as an American stranded in Japan who decides her purpose in life is to become a ramen chef.

perfect for this). Ginger that's grated, rather than chopped, will integrate better into the recipe, but even easier is to buy a jar of minced ginger, which you can find in the Asian foods section of the supermarket. It keeps for months in the refrigerator, so it's always on hand, and it saves you lots of work. The Ginger People (www.gingerpeople.com) have a version I like. Make sure to buy plain minced ginger, not pickled ginger. Jarred minced ginger can be used in any recipe in this book that calls for fresh grated or minced ginger.

> Nissin Foods sells an average of 87.5 billion servings of ramen noodles worldwide each year.

Hoisin Sauce: Made with soybean paste and seasoned with sugar, garlic, and other spices, this thick, sticky glaze has a sweet taste and is great to add flavor and body to sauces, or to use as a glaze, marinade, or dipping sauce. It comes in a jar and will keep for months in the refrigerator.

Oil: Most of the recipes in this book call for either vegetable or canola oil (you can use the two interchangeably). Both of these oils have a neutral flavor and a high smoke point, which means that they won't burn when you're cooking at high temperatures, as you do for frying, sautéing, and stir-frying.

Plum Sauce: A tangy-sweet sauce made of plums, rice vinegar, ginger, and other ingredients, this sauce is excellent used as a condiment or a dipping sauce, particularly for egg rolls or spring rolls.

Ponzu Sauce: This is like a tangier version of soy sauce; in fact, it is really just soy sauce with a citrus flavor. It makes a fantastic dipping sauce and can also add a salty tang to many dishes. You can even just use it on its own to flavor a stir-fry or plain noodles.

Rice Cooking Wine: This fermented, rice-based liquid has a slightly sweet flavor that adds a nice dimension to certain sauces and dishes. There are Chinese and Japanese versions; the Japanese rice wine is called mirin. It typically has a low alcohol content (around 8 to 13 percent). If you don't have any rice wine on hand, you can use dry sherry with similar results. If you prefer not to use alcohol, then use an equal amount of vegetable or chicken stock with a splash of rice vinegar.

Rice Vinegar: If you don't have a bottle of rice vinegar in your pantry, you're missing out. This clear vinegar is more subtly flavored than white wine vinegar and more complex than plain old distilled or cider vinegar. It makes a fantastic vinaigrette, and it's also nice splashed over steamed vegetables. In the Asian foods aisle, you'll see both plain or natural rice vinegar, and seasoned rice vinegar. The seasoned version has added sugar and salt. I prefer the plain; you can always add a little sugar and salt to the recipe if needed. Just make sure not to confuse rice vinegar with rice cooking wine, which contains alcohol and doesn't have the same tartness.

Seaweed Seasoning (nori furikake): This sprinkle, which comes in a glass or plastic shaker, is a ubiquitous condiment on the table in Asian households and restaurants. It comes in several varieties but usually includes shredded dried seaweed, sesame seeds, salt, and sugar, as well as other flavorings like powdered wasabi or dried fish.

Sesame Oil: Another classic Asian ingredient, sesame oil adds a delicious nuttiness to stir-fry sauces, soups, and other dishes. Toasted sesame oil has a more intense flavor. Buy the smallest bottle possible; you only need a teaspoon or so for most recipes (it's added more for flavor than for cooking), and this oil can go rancid quickly. For that reason, store it in a cool, dark cabinet, but not in the refrigerator.

> In one year, Maruchan sells 81 million miles of noodles—enough noodles to extend from Earth to Mars and back again.

Sesame Seeds: These are one of my favorite ways to add flavor, texture, and authenticity to Asian-style dishes, and you'll find them used in recipes throughout this book. Try to find sesame seeds that are already toasted, as they'll have the best flavor and a pretty, golden color. It's also wise to look for a source that sells them in bulk, such as a health food store, as they will be fresher and less expensive than if you buy the ones that come in little spice jars.

Soy Sauce: I use low-sodium soy sauce because I find that it's intensely flavorful without being overly salty. Choose an authentic Japanese brand if possible. Nearly universally, the low-sodium version is the one with the green label.

Sriracha Sauce: This Thai chili sauce is a fantastic condiment for adding a little spice to many of the dishes in this book, as well as just in your day-to-day cooking. It's made with ground chiles, vinegar, garlic, and salt. Use it sparingly until you get a sense of how spicy it is; you can always add more to up the spice quotient of your dish. Keep the bottle in the refrigerator.

Teriyaki Sauce: A sweet, thick, soy-based sauce, this sauce is delicious on noodles, or it can be used as a glaze for meats, tofu, or vegetables.

Thai Chili Sauce: This flavorful Thai sauce is not superhot, but adds a nice dimension of flavor. There's also a sweet version that has even less heat and adds a nice sweet note to a dish. The dishes in this book call for the regular Thai chili sauce, but you can use the sweet one if you prefer.

Tofu: You'll find a wide variety of tofu textures, from silken, which is good for smoothies, to extra-firm, which can be cubed and used in stir-fries. There's also baked tofu, which has a superfirm, meaty texture and is usually flavored. I prefer the fresh tofu that is sold in the refrigerated section, but you can also find shelf-stable cartons of tofu that will keep longer in a pantry. To make extra-firm tofu even firmer for sautéing in a stir-fry, you can press the block of tofu under a weighted plate for 10 to 20 minutes to squeeze out some of its liquid.

Must-Have Kitchenware

To get the best results when making the recipes in this book, you'll need a few basic pieces of cooking equipment. Here are some of the cookware and tools that I reach for again and again when I'm making ramen recipes.

Casserole Dish: Seek out a small covered casserole dish that is around 6 inches in diameter or holds 2 quarts of food. This is the ideal size for the smaller baked dishes. For the dishes in the Feeding a Crowd chapter (page 184), you will need a larger casserole dish, 9 x 13 inches. I like glass or Pyrex casseroles because they heat the food evenly, and they're usually attractive enough to bring to the table.

Cutting Board: A cutting board that is at least 12 inches square will be sufficient for chopping ingredients. I like wood or bamboo, because they will not damage or dull your knife. If you cook with a lot of meat, you might want to consider investing in a set of plastic, color-coded cutting boards or mats so you are using a specific cutting board for each type of food (poultry, meat, fish, and vegetables). This will avoid cross-contamination and will help prevent bacteria from spreading.

Food Processor or Chopper: Several of these recipes call for crushed ramen to use as a crust or in place of bread crumbs. A food processor can crush ramen quickly and easily. You can also use a smaller food chopper, but you might have to work in batches if the entire package of ramen doesn't fit.

Knives: A good-quality chef's knife and paring or utility knife are really all you need to make pretty much all of these recipes. Be sure to keep them sharp either with a home sharpener or by taking them regularly to a sharpening service—a dull knife can be dangerous.

Skillet: A medium (10-inch) nonstick skillet is ideal for making most of the 1- or 2-serving meals in this book. A small (8-inch) skillet is sometimes called for, as well as a large (12-inch) skillet. Try to find skillets that are ovenproof, as some of these recipes require finishing in the oven.

Small Saucepan: I found that a deep, 1-quart saucepan is the ideal size for boiling a single package of ramen noodles. A 2-quart saucepan is more versatile for cooking double batches or cooking the noodles and other ingredients all in one dish.

China, including Hong Kong, consumes the most instant noodles, slurping up a whopping 42.3 billion packages or cups in 2010. The United States ranks fifth, with 3.9 billion packages of ramen noodles eaten in 2010, according to the World Instant Noodles Association.

Strainer: A strainer is essential for rinsing ingredients and draining noodles. I like a small metal mesh strainer with raised feet so you can rest it on the bottom of the sink.

Tongs: A set of tongs will be helpful for cooking meat, stir-frying, tossing salads, mixing noodles with sauces, or lifting noodles out of the boiling water. Try to find a set that has silicone-covered tips so that it won't damage the surface of a nonstick pan.

Whisk: A small whisk can be useful for mixing sauces and beating eggs.

Ramen Techniques

These are some of the techniques you'll see used in the recipes in this book.

How to Cook Ramen Noodles: Fill a small (about 1 quart) saucepan about two-thirds full with water over high heat. When the water comes to a boil, add the ramen cake (break the cake into smaller pieces if you want shorter noodles) and set the timer for 3 minutes, or according to the package directions. Use a spoon to submerge the noodles until they begin to soften and break apart. After 3 minutes, immediately drain the noodles. It's best to cook the noodles just before you will be using them, as they will stick together the longer they sit out. You can cook the noodles for a shorter amount of time if you want slightly firmer noodles.

Instant ramen noodles have proven to be the perfect food for disaster zones. They were distributed to survivors of the 2004 Asian tsunami and again during the 2011 earthquake in Japan.

Crushing Ramen Noodles: When dry ramen noodles are being used as a topping or a mix-in, you can crush them by hand into small pieces. Place the cake of ramen in a bowl and break it apart into chunks. Working with one chunk at a time, use your fingers to break and crumble the dry noodles into the desired-size pieces.

Grinding Ramen Noodles: Finely ground ramen noodles can be used in place of bread crumbs as a topping or in dishes. To grind ramen noodles, break the cake of dry noodles into about eight pieces into the bowl of a food processor. Pulse the processor 8 to 10 times, until the noodles are evenly ground into small particles that resemble oats, coarse cornmeal, or fine bread crumbs, depending on the recipe. If you don't have a food processor, you can place the broken cake of ramen noodles into a zip-top bag, seal the bag (pressing all the air out first), and press a rolling pin over the noodles until they're crushed to a desired consistency.

· · · · · · · ·

SNACKS and STARTERS

When the urge to munch strikes, just reach for a package of ramen. You can really get creative with how you use the noodles to create a wide variety of tasty snacks and appetizers: Pan-fry them into a pancake, roll them up in an edible wrapper, or bake them until they're satisfyingly crunchy.

The snacks on the following pages can be noshed in the middle of the afternoon, passed around at a party, or served as an appetizer at a dinner party. So think outside the bowl and whip up some ramen-based snacks.

THAI BASIL SPRING ROLLS

Noodles tossed with tangy rice vinegar and the fresh flavors of basil, lettuce, and cucumber fill these delicate rolls. If you'd like, tuck a few slices of cooked shrimp or seasoned tofu into each one. You can find the rice paper spring roll wrappers in the Asian section of your supermarket. **Makes 8 spring rolls**

2 packages ramen noodles, any flavor

1 tablespoon rice vinegar

1 head butter lettuce, such as Bibb or Boston, torn into large pieces

16 fresh basil leaves

½ cucumber, peeled, seeded, and cut into 2-inch strips, about ½-inch wide

8 cooked shrimp, sliced, or 8 slices seasoned baked tofu (optional)

8 (8½-inch) sheets rice paper spring roll wrappers

½ cup hoisin sauce

1 tablespoon chopped roasted peanuts

1. Cook the ramen noodles in boiling water for 3 minutes, or according to the package directions (discard the ramen seasoning). Drain the noodles, rinse with cold water, and place in a medium bowl. Sprinkle the noodles with the rice vinegar and toss to coat evenly.

2. Set out all the lettuce, basil, cucumber, and shrimp or tofu, if using, on the countertop, and have a clean work surface in front of you on which to assemble the spring rolls. Fill a shallow dish or a pie pan with warm water.

3. Immerse one spring roll wrapper in the warm water, holding it underneath the water with your fingertips until it is soft and flexible, 30 to 45 seconds. Lift the wrapper out of the water and hold it over the pan of water for a few minutes to let the water drip off. Lay the wrapper on the plate or cutting board.

4. Place about ¼ cup noodles, a piece of lettuce, 2 basil leaves, 3 to 4 strips cucumber, and a few slices of shrimp or tofu, if using, in the middle of the wrapper. Fold about 1 inch of two opposite sides over the filling. Then fold the bottom of the wrapper over the filling to form a rectangular pouch, almost like a business envelope. Tightly pull the top section of the wrapper toward you and roll it over the filling to overlap the other side, pressing slightly to seal the edges.

5. Repeat steps 3 and 4 with the remaining wrappers and ingredients. Place the hoisin sauce in a small serving dish and sprinkle with peanuts. Serve the spring rolls with the hoisin sauce for dipping.

· · · · · · · · ·

PAN-FRIED SCALLION PANCAKE

This quick snack has an appealingly chewy-crunchy texture, and it's best eaten hot, as soon as possible after it comes out of the pan.

Makes 1 (8 to 10-inch) pancake, 1 to 4 servings

1 package ramen noodles, Oriental flavor

3 scallions, light green part only, thinly sliced, divided

1 tablespoon vegetable oil

soy sauce, for dipping

1. Cook the ramen noodles in boiling water for 3 minutes, or according to the package directions (reserve the ramen seasoning). Drain and return to the pot. Sprinkle the noodles with 1 teaspoon of the ramen seasoning (discard the remainder) and most of the scallions, reserving about 1 teaspoon of the scallions for garnish. Toss to coat evenly.

2. Spray a plate with cooking spray. Use clean hands or a spatula to spread the noodles out on the plate and form a flat pancake, about ¾ inch thick, pressing down to compress the noodles.

3. Heat the vegetable oil in a medium nonstick skillet over medium-high heat. When the oil is very hot, slide the pancake into the pan. Cook until the noodles are lightly browned on the underside, 3 to 4 minutes. Carefully flip the pancake over and cook until the second side is browned, about 3 minutes longer. Transfer the pancake to a plate, cut into wedges with a knife or a pizza cutter, and serve immediately with a small dish of soy sauce sprinkled with the reserved scallions.

· · · · · · · · ·

SHRIMP AND EGG PANCAKE

This pancake is denser than the Pan-Fried Scallion Pancake (page 29), almost like a frittata. It makes a substantial snack, or a nice appetizer for a dinner or a party. You can substitute diced seasoned tofu for the shrimp if you prefer. **Makes 1 (8-inch) pancake, 2 to 4 servings**

1 package ramen noodles, any flavor

1 large egg

1 teaspoon soy sauce, plus more for dipping

¼ cup chopped cooked shrimp, canned or thawed frozen

2 tablespoons minced chives

1 tablespoon vegetable oil

1. Cook the ramen noodles in boiling water for 3 minutes, or according to the package directions (discard the ramen seasoning). While the noodles are cooking, whisk the egg and soy sauce together in a small bowl.

2. When the noodles are cooked, drain and place in a medium bowl. Let cool to room temperature. Pour the egg-soy mixture over the noodles, add the shrimp and the chives, and stir to combine.

3. Heat the vegetable oil in a medium nonstick skillet over medium-high heat. When the oil is hot, pour in the noodle mixture and immediately spread the mixture evenly across the pan with a spatula, pressing down to compress. Cook until the egg begins to set and the mixture browns slightly on the underside, about 3 minutes. Carefully flip the pancake over and cook until the egg is completely firm and the second side is lightly browned, 2 to 3 minutes longer.

4. Cut the pancake into wedges and serve with soy sauce for dipping, if desired.

. . . .

CRISPY POTATO PANCAKES WITH CHIVE SOUR CREAM

Ground dry ramen noodles add a nice crunch to traditional potato pancakes, and the seasoning packet adds depth of flavor. The traditional way to serve potato pancakes is with applesauce or sour cream, or both. This recipe doubles (or even triples!) easily if you're cooking for a crowd. **Makes 4 (3 to 4-inch) pancakes**

½ cup reduced-fat sour cream

2 tablespoons minced chives, divided

1 package ramen noodles, onion flavor

2 medium baking potatoes

1 medium onion

1 large egg

salt and pepper

2 tablespoons vegetable oil, or as needed

½ cup applesauce

1. In a small bowl, combine the sour cream, 1 tablespoon chives, and the ramen seasoning. Cover with plastic wrap and refrigerate until needed.

2. Break the ramen noodles into the bowl of a food processor and pulse to grind until they resemble coarse cornmeal.

3. Peel the potatoes and grate them into a colander in the sink. Press down on the potatoes in the colander to squeeze out as much excess water as possible. Transfer the potatoes to a bowl. Peel and grate the onion and combine with the potatoes.

4. In a small bowl, whisk the egg together with a generous pinch each of salt and pepper. Pour the egg mixture into the potato mixture.

5. Heat the vegetable oil in a large nonstick skillet over medium-high heat. The oil should completely coat the bottom of the pan and pool a little bit if you tilt the pan to one side. Drop the pancake batter by the heaping tablespoonful into the hot pan, working in batches if necessary so you don't overcrowd. Press down lightly with a spatula to flatten the pancakes, and fry until the bottoms are browned, 3 to 5 minutes. Flip until the second sides are browned, about 3 minutes longer. Repeat with any remaining pancakes, and serve with the chive sour cream and the applesauce.

· · · · · · · ·

SPICY PEANUT NOODLE WRAPS

This saucy wrap is inspired by a similar sandwich on the menu of one of my favorite restaurants, the Highland Bakery in Atlanta, Georgia. The peanut noodles are on the spicy side, so if you have a sensitive palate, you can cut the amount of red pepper flakes in half. **Makes 2 wraps**

¼ cup smooth peanut butter

2 tablespoons rice vinegar

1 teaspoon sugar

1 tablespoon soy sauce

½ teaspoon grated fresh ginger

½ teaspoon red pepper flakes

½ teaspoon sesame oil

1 tablespoon warm water

1 package ramen noodles, any flavor

1 scallion, dark green part only, thinly sliced

2 teaspoons sesame seeds

2 sandwich wraps or large flour tortillas

½ cup shredded lettuce, such as romaine

1. In a medium bowl, combine the peanut butter, vinegar, sugar, soy sauce, ginger, ½ teaspoon pepper flakes or to taste, sesame oil, and warm water. Stir until smooth, and set aside.

2. Cook the ramen noodles in boiling water for 3 minutes, or according to the package directions (discard the ramen seasoning). Drain the noodles and return to the pot or place in a bowl. Pour the peanut butter sauce over the noodles, sprinkle with the scallion and sesame seeds, and stir to combine. Sauced noodles can be kept covered in the refrigerator for 1 to 2 days.

3. Set the sandwich wraps on a clean work surface. Divide the sesame noodles between the wraps, mounding them in the center of each one. Place half the lettuce on each mound of noodles. Wrap the sandwich by folding two opposite sides of the wraps over the filling, then rolling the rest of the wrap around the filling from bottom to top. Cut each sandwich in half diagonally. Serve immediately.

· · · · · · · · ·

RAMEN PAN PIZZA

With its noodle crust, this is a fun riff on a deep-dish pizza. Get creative with all your favorite toppings, but be sure to have a fork handy because this is one pizza you won't be able to easily eat with your hands! If you don't have an ovenproof skillet, transfer the noodles to a pie pan or a rimmed baking sheet after they've been browned on the stove. Top with the tomato sauce, cheese, and toppings, and then broil.

Makes 2 servings

2 packages ramen noodles, any flavor

1 tablespoon extra-virgin olive oil, divided

1 teaspoon garlic powder

¾ cup canned spaghetti sauce or pizza sauce

¾ cup shredded mozzarella cheese

½ cup to ¾ cup toppings, such as sliced green bell peppers, black olives, pepperoni, or cooked sausage

1. Cook the ramen noodles in boiling water for 3 minutes, or according to the package instructions (discard the ramen seasoning). Drain the noodles, return to the pot, and toss with 1 teaspoon olive oil and garlic powder to coat.

2. Heat the remaining 2 teaspoons olive oil in a medium ovenproof nonstick or cast iron skillet over medium-high heat. Add the ramen noodles to the pan and use a spatula or a wooden spoon to spread the noodles evenly across the pan, pressing down to compress. Cook until the bottom is browned, 3 to 5 minutes.

3. Preheat the broiler. Remove the pan from the heat and evenly spread the tomato sauce over the noodle "crust." Sprinkle the mozzarella evenly over the pizza, and add the toppings of your choice.

4. Place the pizza under the broiler until the cheese melts and the toppings are heated through, about 5 minutes. Cut the pizza into wedges and serve immediately.

• • • • • • • • •

LETTUCE WRAPS

Use leftover chicken or rotisserie chicken as a shortcut ingredient for these tasty lettuce wraps, inspired by Southeast Asian cuisine. A small amount of the seasoning packet is used to flavor the chicken; I think Oriental, chili, or onion flavor would work the best. These wraps feed a crowd as an appetizer or would make a satisfying dinner for three or four people. **Serves 6 to 8 as a snack or appetizer, or 3 to 4 as a meal**

1 package ramen noodles, any flavor

1 cup cooked chicken meat, cut into small chunks

2 teaspoons vegetable oil

3 scallions, white and light green parts, thinly sliced

1 teaspoon minced garlic

1½ cups cabbage slaw mix with carrots

½ cup mung beans

⅓ cup water chestnuts, cut into slivers

⅓ cup plum sauce

2 tablespoons soy sauce

1 teaspoon minced or grated fresh ginger

2 heads butter lettuce, such as Bibb or Boston, cored and separated into leaves

1. Cook the ramen noodles in boiling water for 3 minutes, or according to the package directions. Drain and set aside. Place the chicken in a medium bowl and sprinkle with 1 teaspoon ramen seasoning (discard the remainder). Toss to coat.

2. Heat the vegetable oil in a large nonstick skillet over medium-high heat. Add the chicken and the scallions and sauté until the scallions are soft, about 5 minutes. Add the garlic and cook, stirring constantly, for about 30 seconds.

3. Add the cabbage slaw mix, mung beans, and water chestnuts and cook, stirring occasionally, until the cabbage is wilted and softened, about 5 minutes. Add the noodles to the pan and stir to combine.

4. In a small bowl, stir together the plum sauce, soy sauce, and ginger. Pour the sauce over the mixture in the pan and stir to combine. Cook over medium heat until heated through, 2 to 3 minutes.

5. Transfer the cabbage and noodle mixture to a shallow serving bowl or large platter, and arrange the lettuce leaves on a separate serving platter. To eat, spoon about ¼ cup cabbage and noodle mixture into the center of a lettuce leaf. Roll the edges of the leaf over the filling and eat the roll with your hands.

• • • • • • • •

CHEESY RAMEN-CARROT FRITTERS

A platter of these little bites won't last long at your next get-together—they are positively addictive! You can experiment with the type of cheese you use; mozzarella or Colby would be just as tasty as cheddar. A clean pair of kitchen shears works well to cut the noodles into the right-size mounds. **Makes 8 to 10 fritters**

1 package ramen noodles, any flavor

1 teaspoon vegetable oil

½ cup finely shredded peeled carrots

½ cup shredded sharp cheddar cheese

1. Cook the ramen noodles in boiling water for 3 minutes, or according to the package instructions (discard the ramen seasoning). Drain and place in a medium bowl. Drizzle with the vegetable oil and toss to coat. Let cool to room temperature.

2. Preheat the oven to 350°F. Spray a rimmed baking sheet with cooking spray. Add the carrots and cheese to the noodles and toss to combine. On the prepared baking sheet, form mounds of the noodle mixture, about 1½ inches in diameter, using kitchen shears as necessary to cut the noodles to make the mounds the proper size.

3. Bake the fritters until the tops of the noodles are browned and crunchy, 20 to 25 minutes. Immediately remove the fritters from the baking sheet, using a metal or wooden spatula if they're sticking. Serve immediately.

· · · · · · · · ·

CREAMY MISO DIP

Many of the recipes in this book don't use the seasoning packet that comes with each package of ramen noodles, but this recipe gives you the chance to use some of those wasted packets. This dip is fantastic with celery and carrot sticks, or keep with the Asian theme and serve it with snow peas, bok choy stems, and red bell pepper spears. **Makes ½ cup**

½ cup sour cream   1 miso ramen seasoning packet

In a small bowl, combine the sour cream and ramen seasoning and stir well. Cover with plastic wrap and refrigerate for at least 30 minutes to allow the flavors to meld.

Variation:

For a healthier dip, substitute low-fat Greek-style yogurt for half of the sour cream.

· · · · · · · · ·

TRAIL MIX DROPS

Ramen gives a light crunch to these nourishing little balls, which are part cookie, part energy bar. Keep a couple in your bag or your desk drawer to reenergize yourself during a mid-afternoon slump. I've even been known to eat one or two for breakfast when I'm on the run. The recipe suggests using cashews, but chopped peanuts or almonds would be just as delicious. **Makes 1 dozen**

1 package ramen noodles, any flavor

½ cup rolled oats, old-fashioned or quick cooking

½ cup dried cranberries

⅓ cup coarsely chopped cashews

¾ cup smooth peanut butter

2 tablespoons honey

½ tablespoon light corn syrup

1. In a medium bowl, crumble the ramen noodles, then add the rolled oats, cranberries, and cashews (discard the ramen seasoning). In a small bowl, stir together the peanut butter, honey, and corn syrup until smooth.

2. Line a rimmed baking sheet with parchment paper. Pour the peanut butter mixture into the ramen and oat mixture and use your hands to evenly mix until it forms a thick "dough." Form the mixture into 1-inch balls and place them on the prepared baking sheet. Let the drops rest at room temperature for 1 to 2 hours, or until they firm up, then transfer them to an airtight container. The drops will keep in a container for 2 to 3 days.

* * * * * * * *

BREAKFASTS

Here in the United States, we tend to have a pretty strict definition of breakfast: eggs, pancakes, waffles, toast, cereal, maybe some smoked fish, if we're feeling adventurous. But make room for noodles in your morning meal, whether they're incorporated into a traditional breakfast dish or a recipe that deliciously pushes the breakfast boundaries.

SPINACH-RAMEN BREAKFAST BOWL

Before you dig into this satisfying breakfast, break the yolk of the fried egg and stir it into the noodles. The noodles are flavored with seaweed seasoning (or, in Japanese, nori furikake), made of dried seaweed, sesame seeds, salt, and other flavorings. There are several varieties available, including some made with wasabi (wasabi fumi furikake) and others made with dried fish (seto fumi furikake). These seasonings are worth seeking out at an Asian grocery store or even online. **Serves 1**

½ cup chopped spinach, frozen or fresh

1 package ramen noodles, any flavor

1 tablespoon soy sauce

1 teaspoon seaweed seasoning (*nori furikake*; see above)

1 tablespoon unsalted butter

1 large egg

1. Bring a small saucepan of water to a boil over high heat. Add the spinach and the ramen noodles and boil for 3 minutes (discard the ramen seasoning). Drain and return to the pot. Add the soy sauce and the seasoning and stir to combine.

2. While the noodles cook, in a small nonstick skillet over medium-high heat, melt the butter until it foams. Break the egg into the pan and let it cook, undisturbed, until the white is completely firm but the yolk is still liquid, about 3 minutes. If desired, flip the egg over after about 2 minutes.

3. To serve, transfer the seasoned noodles and spinach into a bowl and top with the fried egg.

• • • • • • • • •

ASPARAGUS AND MOZZARELLA FRITTATA

Serve this easy dish for your next brunch—unlike many egg dishes, it doesn't need to be eaten the minute it's cooked, and it even tastes good at room temperature. For different results, try other kinds of cheese, such as cheddar, smoked Gouda, or crumbled goat cheese. You can also use sautéed mushrooms or spinach (squeeze the excess water out of the spinach first) in place of the asparagus. **Serves 4**

1 cup chopped asparagus (1-inch pieces)

¼ cup water

1 package ramen noodles, any flavor

2 teaspoons extra-virgin olive oil

½ onion, diced

6 large eggs

salt and pepper

1 cup shredded mozzarella cheese (4 ounces)

¼ cup chopped fresh basil

1. In a microwave-safe container with a cover, combine the asparagus and water. Microwave, covered, on high power until tender, about 3 minutes. Drain and set aside.

2. Cook the ramen noodles in boiling water for 3 minutes, or according to the package directions (discard the ramen seasoning). Drain and set aside.

3. In a medium ovenproof nonstick or cast iron skillet, heat the olive oil over medium-high heat. Add the onion and sauté until softened, about 5 minutes. Remove the pan from the heat and add the asparagus. Spread the cooked noodles in an even layer over the asparagus and the onions. In a medium bowl, beat the eggs with a pinch each of salt and pepper. Pour the eggs over the ingredients in the skillet, tilting the pan slightly to cover the mixture evenly. Sprinkle with the mozzarella and the basil.

4. Return the pan to the stove and cook, undisturbed, over medium-high heat until just set, 5 to 7 minutes. The center of the frittata should look moist but shouldn't be jiggly or liquid. If desired, finish the cooking by putting the pan under the broiler until the cheese is browned, 1 to 2 minutes. Serve hot or at room temperature. Leftovers can be stored in the refrigerator, wrapped in aluminum foil, for 1 to 2 days.

• • • • • • • • •

RAMEN-QUILES

Chilaquiles is a popular Mexican breakfast dish that makes use of stale leftover tortillas. The tortilla pieces are fried in oil, then simmered in a tomato-chile sauce, like the sauce that is used on enchiladas. Here, I've used dry ramen noodles, which soften in the sauce. Use traditional Mexican toppings, like diced avocado, fresh cilantro, and queso fresco (a crumbly Mexican cheese that can be found in the ethnic section of most supermarkets, or at a Mexican grocery). Serve this with scrambled eggs and refried beans for a hearty Mexican-style breakfast. **Serves 2 to 3**

1 (15-ounce) can tomato sauce or tomato puree

2 canned chipotle peppers in adobo sauce

½ teaspoon ground cumin

2 packages ramen noodles, any flavor

1 tablespoon vegetable oil

1 small onion, diced

1 avocado, diced

2 tablespoons chopped fresh cilantro

1 ounce queso fresco, crumbled

1. In a blender or food processor, puree the tomato sauce, chipotle peppers, and cumin. In a medium bowl, crumble the ramen noodles (discard the ramen seasoning).

2. In a medium saucepan, heat the vegetable oil over medium heat. Add the onion and the crumbled ramen noodles and sauté, stirring frequently, until the onion is softened and the ramen begins to brown, about 5 minutes.

3. Pour the tomato sauce over the noodles, stir to combine, and simmer over medium-heat until the noodles are just softened but still have a firm texture, 4 to 5 minutes.

4. To serve, divide the noodles among two or three plates and top with the avocado, cilantro, and queso fresco.

· · · · · · · · ·

BACON, EGG, AND NOODLE SCRAMBLE

I love this quick, satisfying breakfast for one. It's fast to make and is an indulgent treat when it's just you and the Sunday paper. Add a cup of coffee and a wedge or two of cantaloupe and you're set. **Serves 1**

1 package ramen noodles, any flavor

2 strips bacon

½ tablespoon unsalted butter

2 large eggs

1 ounce cheddar or Colby cheese, shredded (about 2 tablespoons)

salt and pepper

1. Break the cake of ramen noodles into about 8 pieces and cook them in boiling water for 3 minutes, or according to the package directions (discard the ramen seasoning). Drain and set aside.

2. Put the bacon in a medium nonstick skillet and heat the pan over medium-high heat. Cook the bacon until crisp, 7 to 10 minutes, turning over as needed to evenly cook both sides. Remove the bacon from the pan and drain any excess fat if necessary, so there's no more than about 1 teaspoon of bacon fat left. When the bacon cools, crumble it into pieces and set aside.

3. Add the butter to the hot pan with the bacon fat. When the butter melts, add the noodles and cook, stirring frequently, for 3 to 4 minutes. Meanwhile, beat the eggs lightly in a small bowl with a fork or a whisk. Reduce the heat to low and add the eggs to the pan. Cook, stirring, until the eggs are nearly scrambled, about 4 minutes. Sprinkle the cheese over the eggs and cook, stirring frequently, until the cheese melts. Transfer to a plate or a shallow bowl, season to taste with salt and pepper, sprinkle the crumbled bacon on top, and serve.

. . . .

EGGY SAUSAGE NOODLES

This is just the ticket the morning after a late night out. It's quick and easy to make and is the perfect combination of richness, spiciness, and satisfying carbs. If you're a vegetarian, you can use frozen meatless sausage patties like those from MorningStar Farms. **Serves 1**

1 package ramen noodles, chili flavor

1 tablespoon unsalted butter

1 large egg

2 sausage patties, cooked and roughly chopped

salt and pepper

1. Break the cake of ramen noodles into about 4 pieces and cook them in boiling water for 2½ minutes (reserve the ramen seasoning). Drain, return the noodles to the pot, and immediately add the butter and egg, stirring to coat the noodles with the egg until it is cooked. If there isn't enough heat in the noodles, you can turn the burner back on and cook the mixture over low heat. Stir in the sausage, and season to taste with the salt, pepper, and ¼ teaspoon of the ramen seasoning or to taste. Serve immediately.

• • • • • • • •

RAMEN OMELET

Cooked ramen noodles add substance to an omelet. You can use this delicious combination of bell pepper and mushrooms, or even just use the leftovers from another ramen recipe, such as the Beef and Pepper Bowl (page 115) or Loaded Stir-Fry (page 111). Laughing Cow cheese, a soft, low-fat cheese spread, melts beautifully in an omelet, but you can also use your favorite soft or semisoft cheese, or even a few chunks of cream cheese. **Serves 1**

½ package ramen noodles, any flavor

1 teaspoon vegetable oil or olive oil

¼ cup chopped red bell pepper

¼ cup sliced cremini or white mushrooms

salt and pepper

2 large eggs

1 tablespoon milk or half-and-half

1 tablespoon unsalted butter

1 (¾-ounce) wedge Laughing Cow cheese, any flavor, cut into small pieces

1. Cook the ramen noodles in boiling water for 3 minutes, or according to the package directions (discard the ramen seasoning). Drain and set aside.

2. Heat the oil in a small nonstick skillet over medium-high heat. Add the bell pepper and mushrooms and sauté, stirring occasionally, until soft, about 5 minutes. Season to taste with salt and pepper. Remove the vegetables from the pan and set aside.

3. In a small bowl, whisk together the eggs and milk or half-and-half. Add the butter to the pan and melt over medium-high heat, swirling to coat the pan. Pour the eggs into the pan and tilt the pan to spread evenly. Cook until the eggs are mostly cooked, but the center is still moist, 2 to 3 minutes. Spread the noodles over one-half of the eggs and top with the vegetables and the cheese. Fold the other half over the filling and cook for 1 minute more. Carefully slide the omelet onto a plate and serve immediately.

· · · · · · · · ·

BIRD'S NESTS WITH SPINACH, EGG, AND CHEESE

A fun option for a special brunch or breakfast, these little noodle nests are made in muffin pans and filled with baked eggs. If you like the way the ramen bird's nests turn out, be sure to check out the recipe for Truffled Chicken Salad in Bird's Nests (page 182). Two of these little nests will make a substantial breakfast; at a brunch where you're serving other dishes, you can allow one bird's nest per person.

Serves 2 to 4

1 package ramen noodles, chicken flavor

1 teaspoon sesame oil

½ cup thawed frozen spinach, excess water squeezed out

4 large eggs

¼ cup shredded Colby or cheddar cheese

salt and pepper

1. Preheat the oven to 350°F. Spray 4 cups of a standard muffin pan with cooking spray. Cook the ramen noodles in boiling water for 3 minutes, or according to the package directions (reserve the ramen seasoning). Drain, return to pot, and toss with ½ teaspoon of the ramen seasoning (discard the remainder) and sesame oil. When the noodles are cool enough to handle, press the noodles into the prepared muffin cups, pressing against the bottom and sides of the pan to form a bowl shape that resembles a bird's nest. Bake until the edges turn brown and the noodles begin to harden and turn crisp on the bottom and sides, 20 to 25 minutes. Remove from the oven.

2. Fill each nest with about 2 tablespoons spinach. Being careful to keep the yolk intact, break 1 egg into each nest over the spinach. Return the pan to the oven and bake until the egg white is solid but the yolk still feels liquid, 10 to 12 minutes. Sprinkle each bird's nest with shredded cheese (about 1 tablespoon each) and bake for 1 minute more. Season to taste with salt and pepper, and serve immediately.

• • • • • • • •

JOE'S SPECIAL

New Joe's Restaurant in San Francisco is credited for inventing Joe's Special. This adaptation of the classic breakfast scramble made with spinach, onion, mushrooms, ground beef, and egg is a hearty start to any morning. **Serves 4**

2 packages ramen noodles, beef flavor

6 large eggs

2 tablespoons water

¼ teaspoon cracked black pepper

1 tablespoon olive oil

2 tablespoons unsalted butter, divided

4 large cremini mushrooms, chopped

½ large sweet onion, diced

1 teaspoon minced garlic

8 ounces lean ground beef

½ teaspoon dried oregano, crushed

½ teaspoon dried basil, crushed

1 teaspoon Tabasco sauce

1 cup tomato sauce

1 (8-ounce) bag baby spinach

¼ cup grated Parmesan cheese

1. Cook the ramen noodles in boiling water for 3 minutes, or according to the package directions (reserve the ramen seasoning). Drain and set aside.

2. In a medium bowl, whisk together the eggs, water, and black pepper. Set aside.

3. Heat the olive oil and 1 tablespoon butter in a large skillet over medium-high heat. Add the mushrooms and sauté until the mushrooms begin to brown, about 3 minutes. Add the onion and cook, stirring occasionally, until the onion is translucent, about 5 minutes. Add the garlic and cook, stirring constantly, about 30 seconds. Push the mixture to the side of the pan.

4. Add the ground beef and about half of the ramen seasoning. Cook, stirring occasionally, until the beef begins to brown, 7 to 10 minutes. Combine the beef with the mushroom mixture. Add the remaining ramen seasoning, oregano, basil, and 1 teaspoon Tabasco sauce or to taste, and stir to combine. Continue to cook until the beef is mostly cooked through, about 3 minutes. Add the tomato sauce and spinach, and stir to combine. Cover the pan and cook until the spinach is wilted, about 3 minutes. Uncover the pan, add the noodles, and stir to combine. Cook until the noodles have warmed through, about 2 minutes longer. Set aside, and cover with a lid or aluminum foil to keep warm.

5. Heat the remaining 1 tablespoon butter in a medium nonstick skillet over medium-high heat. Add the egg mixture and cook, stirring constantly to scramble the eggs, about 4 to 5 minutes.

6. Fold the eggs into the beef mixture.

7. Divide the mixture between four bowls. Top each with 1 tablespoon Parmesan cheese and serve.

. . . .

QUICHE LORRAINE

This version of quiche Lorraine has a ground-ramen crust and is baked and served in individual ramekins. Serve with fresh fruit and coffee to start any day on the right foot. If you end up with extra dough, make pie-crust cookies: Press the dough scraps into a ball and roll out to ¼ inch thick. Brush with melted butter and sprinkle with cinnamon and sugar. Bake at 350°F until golden brown, about 15 minutes. **Serves 2**

1 package ramen noodles, any flavor

½ cup all-purpose flour

2 tablespoons unsalted butter

5 tablespoons ice water, divided

2 large eggs plus 1 egg white

½ cup heavy cream

¼ teaspoon ground nutmeg

¼ teaspoon salt

1 scallion, minced

½ cup diced Black Forest ham

½ cup shredded Gruyère cheese

1. Preheat the oven to 350°F.

2. Break the ramen noodles into the bowl of a food processor and pulse to grind into a fine powder. Measure out ½ cup ground ramen and place in a medium bowl. Discard the remaining ramen noodles and the ramen seasoning. Add the flour and stir to combine. Cut the butter into small cubes and add to the bowl. Using two knives or a pastry cutter, cut the butter into the ramen and flour mixture until it is about the size of small peas. Add 2 tablespoons ice water and begin to combine the dough. Add the remaining 3 tablespoons ice water and continue to combine, until the dough just comes together. It will be sticky at this point.

3. Lightly flour a cutting board. Divide the dough into two balls and flatten each ball into a disk. Using a rolling pin, roll out each disk to approximately ¼ inch thick. Line the bottom and sides of two individual large ramekins (about 5 inches in diameter) with dough, trimming off any excess. Bake for 15 minutes.

4. While the crust is baking, put the eggs and egg white in a medium bowl and whisk until combined. Add the cream, nutmeg, and ¼ teaspoon salt or to taste, and whisk to combine. Stir in the scallion.

5. Remove the ramekins from the oven. Being careful to not burn yourself, add 2 tablespoons each of the ham and cheese to each ramekin. Pour the egg mixture over each quiche until full. Discard any remaining egg mixture. Return the ramekins to the oven and bake until the quiche is fully cooked and the top is lightly browned, 35 to 40 minutes. Remove from the oven and cool for 5 minutes before serving.

• • • • • • • • •

RAMEN-CRUSTED CINNAMON FRENCH TOAST

My kids beg for seconds of this version of French toast when I make it for them on the weekends. The bread gets a little crunch from a coating of sweetened dry ramen noodles, and this dish is great with maple syrup, but try it with fruit sauce instead for a twist. Bread that's slightly stale makes the best French toast, because it's dried out enough to absorb the egg custard. If your bread is still moist, you could put it in a warm (200°F) oven until the center of the bread starts to dry out a little, 5 to 10 minutes. **Serves 3**

1 tablespoon unsalted butter, plus more for cooking

1 teaspoon sugar

1½ teaspoons ground cinnamon, divided

1 package ramen noodles, any flavor

4 large eggs

¼ cup half-and-half or whole milk

1 teaspoon vanilla extract

pinch salt

6 slices day-old crusty bread

1. In a small nonstick skillet, melt 1 tablespoon butter. Sprinkle the sugar and 1 teaspoon cinnamon into the pan and stir to melt the sugar. Crumble the ramen noodles into the pan and cook, stirring constantly, for about 5 minutes (discard the ramen seasoning). Transfer the ramen to a food processor and pulse until finely ground. Spread the ramen mixture in a shallow dish, such as a pie pan.

2. In a medium bowl, whisk together the eggs, half-and-half or milk, vanilla, remaining ½ teaspoon cinnamon, and salt.

3. Heat a griddle or a large skillet over medium-high heat. Coat the cooking surface lightly with butter. Dip one slice of bread into the egg mixture, hold it over the bowl to let the excess drip off, then roll the bread in the ramen mixture to coat it completely, pressing the ramen noodles into the bread to make them stick. Repeat with the remaining bread slices. Working in batches if necessary, put the crusted French toast on the hot griddle or skillet and cook until browned, about 4 minutes on each side. Serve immediately.

● ● ● ● ● ● ● ●

RAMEN BREI

Jewish people often make a breakfast dish called matzoh brei from the unleavened cracker-bread eaten during the holiday of Passover. Moistened matzoh is scrambled with eggs and served either sprinkled with salt and pepper, or sweetened with maple syrup, and uncooked ramen noodles can be used in the same way. If you'd like to try it savory, omit the cinnamon and serve your ramen brei with salt and pepper, and maybe a dash of hot sauce. **Serves 2**

1 package ramen noodles, any flavor
¾ cup milk
2 large eggs

½ teaspoon ground cinnamon
1 tablespoon unsalted butter
maple syrup, to serve

1. In a small bowl, break the ramen noodles into bite-size chunks (discard the ramen seasoning). Pour the milk over the noodles so they are nearly completely covered and let sit, stirring occasionally, for 10 minutes.

2. Break the eggs into a second small bowl and whisk until smooth. Add the cinnamon and stir to combine.

3. Melt the butter in a small nonstick skillet over medium-high heat, tilting to coat the bottom of the pan with the butter. Drain the excess milk from the ramen noodles and add them to the pan. Add the eggs and cook, stirring constantly with a rubber spatula, until the eggs are completely cooked and the ramen is lightly browned, about 5 minutes. Serve hot, drizzled with maple syrup or pancake syrup.

• • • • • • • • •

SOUPS

Ramen noodles are at their most traditional when swimming in a flavorful soup—but that doesn't mean you can't have fun and get creative. After all, think of all the classic soup recipes around the world that include noodles, from chicken noodle to minestrone. On a chilly night, brew up one of these satisfying recipes for an easy, warming supper.

VIETNAMESE NOODLE SOUP

One of my favorite soups of all time is pho, a fragrant broth with chewy noodles and plenty of fresh toppings like crisp mung beans, pungent herbs, and tangy lime wedges. Most Vietnamese cooks and restaurants jealously guard their recipe for pho's unctuous, complexly flavored broth, but I've done my best to replicate the spicy, meaty, rich flavor.

Serves 2

4 ounces flank steak or hanger steak

4 cups beef broth

½ onion, thinly sliced

1 cinnamon stick

1 (2-inch) piece fresh lemongrass, halved lengthwise

1 (1-inch) piece fresh ginger, peeled and sliced

2 star anise pods

½ teaspoon ground coriander

2 teaspoons fish sauce

1 tablespoon brown sugar (optional)

1 package ramen noodles, any flavor

Garnishes:

fresh mung beans

lime wedges

hoisin sauce

Sriracha sauce

fresh basil leaves

fresh mint leaves

1. Trim the steak of excess fat. Slice across the grain as thinly as possible; to get thinner slices, place the beef in the freezer for 20 to 30 minutes to firm it before cutting. In a medium saucepan, combine the beef broth, onion, cinnamon, lemongrass, ginger, star anise, coriander, and fish sauce. Bring to a boil over medium-high heat, then reduce the heat to low and simmer for 30 minutes. Strain out and discard the solids, then return the broth to the saucepan and taste it, adding the brown sugar, if desired. Add the ramen noodles to the broth and simmer for 3 minutes (discard the ramen seasoning).

2. To serve, arrange the garnishes on a platter. Divide the beef between two soup bowls, draping it in the bottom. Bring the broth and noodles to a boil, then immediately divide it between the bowls, pouring it over the beef. The hot broth will cook the beef. Spoon the soup into the bowls. Serve with the platter of garnishes.

· · · · · · · · ·

MISO RAMEN

My four-year-old daughter loves the miso soup that's served at sushi restaurants. She hunts in her bowl for every last chunk of tofu and eagerly slurps up the rich, salty broth. Although it's not quite as good as the real thing, I've started buying packets of instant miso soup and doctoring them up with the traditional tofu and scallions, plus ramen noodles to make it a little more substantial. Cross some culinary boundaries and serve this with a grilled-cheese sandwich, or perhaps with a sandwich made from Chinese Chicken Salad (page 85) for a nice lunch. **Serves 2**

2 cups water

1 package miso soup mix (enough for 2 servings)

2 scallions, chopped

½ cup diced soft tofu

¼ cup sliced cremini mushrooms or shiitakes with stems discarded (optional)

1 package ramen noodles, any flavor

1. In a medium saucepan over medium-high heat, bring the water to a simmer. Add the soup mix, scallions, tofu, and mushrooms, if using, and stir to combine. Add the ramen noodles and simmer for 3 minutes (discard the ramen seasoning). Serve immediately.

. . . .

THAI COCONUT-LEMONGRASS SOUP

When I'm under the weather, the Thai soup called tom kha kai *is as restorative as chicken noodle soup. The ramen noodles help soak up the deliciously rich broth and make this into a substantial one-pot meal. You can use light coconut milk in this recipe, but it won't be as rich or as thick.* **Serves 2**

1 (13½-ounce) can coconut milk

1 (2-inch) piece fresh lemongrass

1 teaspoon grated fresh ginger

1 teaspoon Thai chili sauce

2 tablespoons fish sauce

1 tablespoon brown sugar

1 boneless, skinless chicken breast, trimmed of excess fat, cut into bite-size pieces

1 package ramen noodles, any flavor

juice of 1 lime

1 tablespoon chopped cilantro

1. In a small saucepan over medium-high heat, combine the coconut milk, lemongrass, ginger, chili sauce, fish sauce, and brown sugar. Bring to a simmer, then add the chicken and simmer, stirring occasionally, until the chicken is cooked through, about 5 minutes.

2. Add the ramen noodles and simmer for 3 minutes longer (discard the ramen seasoning). Stir in the lime juice to taste. Serve in bowls garnished with the cilantro.

Variation:

Use 2 boneless, skinless chicken thighs instead of the breast meat. Thigh meat is a little richer and more flavorful.

• • • • • • • •

ASIAN CHICKEN NOODLE SOUP

Scallions, soy sauce, and cilantro give this otherwise traditional chicken soup recipe an Asian edge. It's a nice quick lunch and goes well with a toasted cheese sandwich. **Serves 2**

2 teaspoons extra-virgin olive oil

1 carrot, peeled, halved lengthwise, and thinly sliced into half-moons

1 rib celery, thinly sliced

2 scallions, white and light green parts, thinly sliced

1 boneless, skinless chicken thigh, cut into bite-size pieces

2 cups water

1 package ramen noodles, chicken flavor

½ teaspoon soy sauce

1 tablespoon chopped fresh cilantro

1. In a small saucepan, heat the olive oil over medium-high heat. Add the carrot, celery, and scallions and sauté, stirring frequently, until the vegetables are tender, 5 to 7 minutes. Add the chicken and sauté until it's just lightly browned, about 1 minute.

2. Add the water and the ramen seasoning. Bring to a simmer over medium-high heat, then reduce heat to medium-low and simmer until the chicken is cooked through, 5 to 7 minutes. Add the ramen noodles and cook until the noodles are tender, about 3 minutes. Stir in the soy sauce. Serve in bowls, garnished with the cilantro.

● ● ● ● ● ● ● ● ●

LENTIL NOODLE SOUP

I'm a big fan of cooking with lentils. They have the same heartiness as beans, but they don't require lengthy soaking and cooking times. This little soup is just right for an autumn lunch. You can even pack it in a thermos for work or to take on a hike. **Serves 2 to 3**

2 teaspoons extra-virgin olive oil

2 medium carrots, peeled and diced

1 rib celery, diced

1 small onion, diced

3 cups water, divided

1 package ramen noodles, beef flavor

½ cup green lentils

salt and pepper

grated Parmesan cheese, for garnish

1. In a small saucepan, heat the olive oil over medium heat. Add the carrots, celery, and onion, and sauté, stirring occasionally, until soft, about 7 minutes. Stir in 2 cups water, the ramen seasoning, and the lentils. Bring to a boil, then cover partially so that just a crack remains. Reduce the heat to medium-low and simmer until the lentils are tender, about 20 minutes.

2. Add the remaining 1 cup of water and bring to a simmer over medium heat. Break the ramen noodles into 4 to 6 pieces and add them to the soup. Simmer until the noodles are tender, about 3 minutes. Season to taste with salt and pepper. Serve in bowls with Parmesan cheese sprinkled on top.

• • • • • • • • •

CHICKEN CURRY SOUP

This soup is a variation of panang curry, one of the mildest of the Thai curries. Don't be daunted by the long list of ingredients; it's well worth the extra chopping, and if you have leftover veggies, you can use them the next day to make a stir-fry. **Serves 2 to 4**

1 package ramen noodles, chicken flavor

2 tablespoons vegetable oil, plus more if needed

8 ounces boneless, skinless chicken breast, cut into bite-size pieces

1 cup shiitake mushrooms, stemmed and sliced into thirds

1 shallot, chopped

1 large clove garlic, minced

1 large carrot, peeled and chopped

½ small red bell pepper, chopped

4 ounces green beans, trimmed and cut into 1-inch pieces

1 teaspoon minced or grated fresh ginger

3 tablespoons red curry paste

1 (14-ounce) can light coconut milk

1 cup chicken stock or broth

1 baby bok choy, chopped

1 cup bean sprouts

1 tablespoon minced cilantro

½ lime, cut into wedges

¼ cup chopped salted peanuts

1. Cook the ramen noodles in boiling water for 3 minutes, or according to the package directions (reserve the ramen seasoning). Drain and set aside.

2. Heat the vegetable oil in a medium saucepan over medium-high heat. Add the chicken and sauté just until browned on all sides, about 4 minutes. Transfer the chicken to a bowl or plate and set aside. Add the mushrooms to the pan and cook until browned, about 7 minutes. Remove from the pan and add to the chicken.

3. If needed, add 1 or 2 teaspoons more oil to the pan. Add the shallots and cook, stirring occasionally, until translucent, about 5 minutes. Add the garlic and cook, stirring constantly, about 30 seconds. Add the carrot, bell pepper, and green beans, and cook for 3 minutes. Add the chicken and mushrooms back to the pan, as well as the ginger, and stir to combine. Cook for 2 minutes. Add the ramen seasoning and 3 tablespoons curry paste or to taste, and stir to combine. Add the coconut milk and chicken stock or broth, and stir to combine. Bring to a simmer and immediately reduce the heat so it is just barely simmering. Cook for 5 minutes.

4. Add the bok choy and bean sprouts. Cover, and cook for 3 minutes. Uncover, add the cilantro, and stir to combine.

5. Divide the noodles among two to four bowls. Ladle broth into each bowl. Squeeze fresh lime over each bowl of soup and garnish each with peanuts.

• • • • • • • •

MINESTRONE SOUP

This soup makes a complete meal when served with Italian bread and a fresh green salad. For a heartier version, add 8 ounces cooked ground beef or turkey. Or, to make this completely vegetarian, substitute vegetable stock or broth for the beef stock or broth and eliminate the ramen noodle seasoning packet. **Serves 2 to 4**

2 tablespoons vegetable oil

½ medium onion, chopped

2 ribs celery, chopped

2 carrots, peeled, quartered, and chopped

1 small red bell pepper, chopped

4 ounces green beans, trimmed and cut into 1-inch pieces

1 small zucchini, quartered and chopped

2 large cloves garlic, minced

2 tablespoons tomato paste

1 tablespoon dried basil

1½ teaspoons dried oregano

1 package ramen noodles, beef flavor

1 (14-ounce) can diced tomatoes

1 (14-ounce) can kidney beans, rinsed and drained

2 cups beef stock or broth

1 cup water

1 bay leaf

2 tablespoons minced fresh parsley

¼ cup grated Parmesan cheese

1. Heat the vegetable oil in a large saucepan over medium-high heat. Add the onion, celery, and carrot and sauté, stirring occasionally, until the onion is translucent, 4 to 5 minutes. Add the bell pepper, green beans, and zucchini, and cook for about 2 minutes to soften. Add the garlic and cook, stirring constantly, about 30 seconds. Add the tomato paste, basil, oregano, and ramen seasoning, and stir to combine. Add the tomatoes, kidney beans, beef stock or broth, water, and bay leaf, and stir to combine. Bring to a simmer, then reduce the heat to low, cover, and cook for 20 minutes.

2. Remove the bay leaf. Break the ramen noodles into quarters and stir into the soup. Cook for 3 minutes and stir again to break up the noodles. Add the parsley, stir to combine, and cook for 2 minutes longer.

3. Ladle the soup into bowls. Garnish with Parmesan cheese.

● ● ● ● ● ● ● ● ●

TOMATO SOUP WITH PARMESAN RAMEN CROUTONS

A good bowl of tomato soup is indeed one of life's greatest pleasures. There are some great canned varieties on the market, but every so often I like to make my own. It's not difficult, and the flavor is fresher and more complex than what you can get from canned. Float a Parmesan Ramen Crouton on top for a nice texture contrast and visual appeal. This soup is great alongside a BLT or a grilled cheese sandwich.

Serves 2

2 Parmesan Ramen Croutons (page 79)

1 tablespoon unsalted butter

½ medium onion, chopped

1 carrot, peeled and chopped

1 rib celery, chopped

1 clove garlic, chopped

1 (14-ounce) can crushed tomatoes

2 cups water

1 bay leaf

¼ cup heavy cream

salt and pepper

1. First, make the croutons (reserve the ramen seasoning).

2. In a medium saucepan, melt the butter over medium heat. Add the onion, carrot, and celery and sauté, stirring occasionally, until the vegetables are tender, about 10 minutes. Add the garlic and sauté, stirring constantly, about 30 seconds.

3. Add the tomatoes, the reserved ramen seasoning, water, and bay leaf. Bring to a simmer, then reduce the heat and simmer until the vegetables are very tender, 20 to 25 minutes. Remove the bay leaf.

4. Allow the soup to cool slightly, then puree in a blender or a food processor, or use an immersion blender directly in the pan. Return the soup to the pan, stir in the cream, and season to taste with salt and pepper. To serve, ladle soup into two bowls and float a Parmesan Ramen Crouton on top of each one.

• • • • • • • •

SPICY BEEF AND MUSHROOM STEW

This hearty, beefy stew has an addictively spicy edge thanks to the ramen seasoning packet. The recipe calls for wine to deglaze the pan; the liquid loosens all the flavorful browned bits from the pan so they can mix into the sauce or broth. If you would prefer not to use alcohol, you can use a tablespoon of balsamic vinegar mixed with a tablespoon of beef broth. **Serves 2**

2 teaspoons extra-virgin olive oil

½ onion, cut in half and sliced

1 rib celery, thinly sliced

1 carrot, peeled, halved lengthwise, and thinly sliced

1 cup quartered cremini or white mushrooms

6 ounces flank steak or hanger steak, cut into bite-size pieces

2 tablespoons red wine

1 cup beef stock or broth

1 cup water

1 package ramen noodles, chili flavor

1. Heat the olive oil in a medium saucepan over medium-high heat. Add the onion, celery, and carrot and sauté, stirring occasionally, until the vegetables are softened, about 5 minutes. Add the mushrooms and steak and sauté, stirring, until the steak is browned and the mushrooms are soft, 2 to 3 minutes. Add the wine and sauté, scraping the browned bits off the bottom of the pan, until most of the liquid has evaporated, 1 to 2 minutes.

2. Add the stock or broth, water, and ramen seasoning. Bring to a simmer, then reduce the heat to low and simmer for 10 minutes. Break the noodles into pieces, submerge them in the stew, and cook until soft, about 3 minutes. Serve immediately.

· · · · · · · · ·

SALADS

Cooked or uncooked, ramen noodles are always a handy ingredient to keep on hand for making salads. They can add crunch to slaw or green salads, especially as a sprinkle seasoned with cheese and dried herbs. Cooked and chilled, they make delicious noodle salads that are perfect to pack in a lunch for work or school, or to tote to a picnic or a potluck. As I was testing these salads, I shared many of them at neighborhood get-togethers and was pleasantly surprised by how many requests I got for the recipes!

RAMEN ROMANO SPRINKLE

You'll find a plethora of uses for this savory, crunchy topping. Sprinkle it on salads, baked potatoes, pastas, or soups. I also like it as a topping for baked casseroles like macaroni and cheese or green bean casserole.

Makes ¾ cup

1 package ramen noodles, any flavor

2 tablespoons grated Romano or Parmesan cheese

1 teaspoon dried oregano

½ teaspoon salt

1 tablespoon unsalted butter, melted

1. Preheat a toaster oven or conventional oven to 350°F and line a rimmed baking sheet with parchment paper. In a small bowl, crumble the ramen noodles into small bits (discard the ramen seasoning). Stir in the cheese, oregano, and salt. Drizzle with the butter and stir to coat.

2. Spread the mixture evenly on the prepared baking sheet. Bake until browned, about 5 to 8 minutes, stirring halfway. Cool completely. Store in an airtight container for 1 to 2 days.

• • • • • • • •

PARMESAN RAMEN CROUTONS

Use the crunchy cake of dry ramen noodles in place of bread to make an unusual crouton that's perfect on a salad, such as Caesar Salad with Parmesan Ramen Croutons (page 82) or floating atop a bowl of soup, like Tomato Soup with Parmesan Ramen Croutons (page 74). Actually, it's hard not to just eat these croutons on their own. **Makes 8 to 12 croutons**

½ teaspoon garlic powder

1 tablespoon grated Parmesan cheese

1 package ramen noodles, any flavor

2 tablespoons unsalted butter, melted, divided.

1. Preheat a toaster oven or conventional oven to 350°F and line a rimmed baking sheet with parchment paper. In a small bowl, stir together the garlic powder and Parmesan cheese.

2. Carefully break the two layers of the ramen cake apart (discard the ramen seasoning). Then break each half into 4 to 6 large pieces. Arrange the pieces on the prepared baking sheet and brush them with 1 tablespoon melted butter. Sprinkle half of the Parmesan mixture over the cakes. Bake for 5 minutes. Remove from the oven, turn each crouton over with a pair of tongs or a spatula, and brush them with the remaining 1 tablespoon butter and sprinkle with the rest of the Parmesan mixture. Bake until the croutons are lightly browned, about 5 minutes longer.

• • • • • • • • •

GREEN SALAD WITH RAMEN ROMANO SPRINKLE AND BALSAMIC VINAIGRETTE

Ever since I discovered how easy it is to make your own salad dressing, I haven't purchased a single bottle of the store-bought stuff. This salad is quick and easy to make; keep the ingredients on hand so you can make one to go with dinner any day. **Serves 2 to 4**

1 teaspoon Dijon mustard

½ cup balsamic vinegar

¼ teaspoon kosher salt

pinch of black pepper

¼ cup extra-virgin olive oil

1 (5-ounce) package prewashed salad greens, like baby spinach, arugula, or mixed greens

½ cup dried cranberries

½ cup crumbled blue cheese or goat cheese

¼ cup Ramen Romano Sprinkle (page 78)

1. In a small bowl, whisk together the mustard and the vinegar until smooth. Stir in the salt and pepper. While whisking, drizzle in the olive oil.

2. Place the salad greens in a serving bowl. Whisk the salad dressing to re-emulsify, then pour it over the greens and toss to coat. Sprinkle the cranberries, the cheese, and the sprinkle over the top before serving.

Variations:

Experiment with different varieties of mustard, vinegar, and oil to change the flavor of the dressing. For instance:

- Honey mustard, champagne vinegar, and walnut oil

- Tarragon mustard, red wine vinegar, and grapeseed oil

- Wasabi mustard, rice wine vinegar, canola oil, and 1 teaspoon sesame oil

• • • • • • • • •

CAESAR SALAD WITH PARMESAN RAMEN CROUTONS

My college friend HeeJai helped broaden my culinary horizons after I graduated from a Midwestern state school. When I followed her to live in Chicago, she introduced me to Thai noodles, sushi, and Indian food, and she and her sisters taught me lessons about cooking and entertaining that still influence me today. The dressing for this Caesar salad is adapted from one she often made for dinner parties. It's a bit garlicky, but I love the fresh, bright flavor and the easy, no-mess way that it's made in a zip-top bag. **Serves 4**

1 clove garlic, minced

2 tablespoons extra-virgin olive oil

2 tablespoons plain yogurt

2 tablespoons mashed anchovies

1 dash Worcestershire sauce

1 tablespoon fresh lemon juice

1 head romaine lettuce, torn into bite-size pieces

1 recipe Parmesan Ramen Croutons (page 79)

1. In a 1-gallon zip-top bag, combine the garlic, olive oil, yogurt, anchovies, and Worcestershire sauce. Seal the bag and use your fingers on the outside of the bag to mash the ingredients together.

2. Just before serving, add the lemon juice and mash to combine. Add the lettuce to the bag, seal it, and shake to coat the leaves with dressing.

3. To serve, divide the dressed lettuce among four chilled salad plates. Top with Parmesan Ramen Croutons.

• • • • • • • • •

COLD NOODLE SALAD WITH GRILLED BEEF

This is by far one of my favorite recipes in this book—it's the perfect combination of grilled beef, red onions, and chewy noodles dressed in a tangy seasoning, garnished with fresh cilantro. It makes a fantastic main-course salad for dinner or lunch. This dish is easy to make in a grill pan, but if you have an outdoor grill (or an electric countertop grill), by all means, use it! **Serves 2**

8 ounces flank steak, trimmed of excess fat

1 red onion, halved and sliced

2 tablespoons soy sauce

1 package ramen noodles, beef flavor

2 tablespoons rice vinegar

½ teaspoon Dijon mustard

1 tablespoon canola oil

2 tablespoons ground peanuts

2 tablespoons chopped fresh cilantro leaves

1. Heat a grill or a grill pan over high heat. Put the flank steak and red onion in a bowl and drizzle with the soy sauce, tossing with tongs or a fork to coat. When the grill or the pan is very hot, spray it with cooking spray or brush it with vegetable oil and put the beef and the onions on the grill or in the pan. Cook for 2 to 3 minutes, then flip the beef and turn the onions. Cook 3 minutes longer, then transfer the beef and the onions to a plate and keep warm by covering them loosely with aluminum foil.

2. Cook the ramen noodles in boiling water for 3 minutes, or according to the package directions (reserve the ramen seasoning). While the noodles are cooking, make the dressing. In a large bowl, whisk together the rice vinegar, mustard, and ¼ teaspoon of the ramen seasoning. While whisking, drizzle in the oil. When the noodles are finished cooking, drain in a colander and rinse with cold water until cool. Transfer the noodles to the bowl with the dressing and toss to coat.

3. To serve, slice the beef into thin strips diagonally. Divide the noodles between two plates or shallow bowls. Place the beef and the onions on the noodles and garnish with peanuts and fresh cilantro.

HOW TO POACH CHICKEN

Poaching is a great method to achieve tender, moist chicken meat. Use poached chicken to make chicken salad, such as Chinese Chicken Salad (page 85) or Truffled Chicken Salad in Bird's Nests (page 182), or in sandwiches.

1. Place a chicken in a small pot or deep saucepan. Cover the chicken with chicken broth, enough to completely submerge the chicken. Bring to a boil over high heat, then reduce the heat, cover, and simmer until the chicken is cooked through, about 30 minutes. The chicken's internal temperature should measure 165°F on a meat thermometer. Remove the chicken from the broth and let it cool until it's no longer too hot to handle. Use a knife to slice off the breasts and the legs and use your fingers to remove and discard the skin and pull the meat off the bones. Use a knife to chop the chicken according to the recipe instructions. The cooled chicken broth can be skimmed of excess fat and reserved to use in any recipe that calls for chicken broth or stock.

CHINESE CHICKEN SALAD

Studded with sweet Mandarin oranges, this salad has a retro feel, like something that "ladies who lunch" would have enjoyed after a morning of shopping. Serve it on a bed of lettuce, or on a croissant or brioche bun. A rotisserie chicken will provide roughly the right amount of meat; just carve it up and remove the skin. You can also poach some chicken; see page 84. **Serves 6 to 8**

1 package ramen noodles, any flavor

1/3 cup sliced or slivered almonds

1 tablespoon unsalted butter

1 teaspoon five-spice powder

1 pound cooked chicken meat, chopped

2 ribs celery, diced

2 scallions, chopped

1/2 cup chopped water chestnuts

3/4 cup drained Mandarin oranges

1/4 cup mayonnaise

salt and pepper

1. Crumble the ramen noodles into a small bowl (discard the ramen seasoning) and add the almonds. Melt the butter in a small nonstick skillet over medium-high heat. Pour the melted butter into the noodle mixture and stir to coat. Sprinkle with the five-spice powder and stir to distribute. Pour the mixture into the pan and sauté over medium heat, stirring frequently, until the noodles and nuts begin to brown, about 5 minutes. Remove from the heat and let cool.

2. In a bowl, combine the chicken, celery, scallions, water chestnuts, and Mandarin oranges. Stir in the mayonnaise and season to taste with salt and pepper. Just before serving, stir in the cooled ramen and nut mixture.

• • • • • • • • •

SOUTHERN-STYLE SLAW

In the Southern city in which I live, a version of this cabbage-ramen slaw shows up at many potlucks and picnics. Since it doesn't contain mayonnaise, it will withstand sitting out on a warm day better than potato salad or creamy coleslaw. Just make sure to stir in the dry noodles just before serving, as they will get a little soggy after they've sat in the dressing for a while. Tip: To get the perfect size of crumbles of dried ramen noodles, put them in a sealed zip-top bag. Lay the bag on the countertop, and run a rolling pin back and forth over it a few times.

Serves 8 to 10

²/₃ cup cider vinegar

¼ cup extra-virgin olive oil

¼ cup brown sugar

1 tablespoon poppy seeds

salt and pepper

1 (16-ounce) package cabbage slaw mix with carrots

1 cup chopped broccoli

3 scallions, chopped

¼ cup crushed peanuts

1 package ramen noodles, any flavor

1. In a small bowl, whisk together the cider vinegar, olive oil, and brown sugar, stirring until the sugar is dissolved. Stir in the poppy seeds and season to taste with salt and pepper.

2. In a serving bowl, combine the cabbage slaw mix, broccoli, and scallions. Pour the dressing over the coleslaw and toss to combine completely. Crush the ramen noodles (discard the ramen seasoning). Just before serving, add the peanuts and ramen noodles and toss to distribute them evenly.

• • • • • • • •

ASIAN CABBAGE SLAW

The Asian version of classic ramen-cabbage slaw features napa cabbage, snow peas, cilantro, almonds, and a tangy rice vinegar dressing. It adds a sophisticated touch to a fancy picnic. **Serves 8**

1 head napa cabbage, shredded (about 4 cups)

½ cup toasted sliced almonds

1½ cups snow peas, sliced crosswise diagonally

⅓ cup chopped fresh cilantro

3 scallions, sliced

⅓ cup seasoned rice vinegar, or regular rice vinegar plus 2 teaspoons sugar

1 teaspoon yellow mustard

½ teaspoon sesame oil

2 tablespoons sesame seeds

1 package ramen noodles, any flavor

1. In a large bowl, combine the cabbage, almonds, snow peas, cilantro, and scallions. In a small bowl, whisk together the rice vinegar, mustard, and sesame oil. Drizzle the dressing over the cabbage mixture. Add the sesame seeds and toss to combine all the ingredients.

2. Crumble the ramen noodles into a small bowl (discard the ramen seasoning). Just before serving, stir in the crumbled ramen noodles.

· · · · · · · · ·

CHILLY GINGER-CUCUMBER SALAD

Cool and refreshing, this simple salad makes a great accompaniment to homemade sushi, grilled tuna, or fried chicken. It's also nice to make for a picnic or a potluck—just double or triple the recipe. **Serves 2 to 4**

¼ cup rice vinegar

1 teaspoon grated fresh ginger

1 teaspoon canola oil

1 package ramen noodles, any flavor

1 cucumber, peeled, seeded, and diced

1 scallion, light green and dark green parts only, sliced

1 tablespoon sesame seeds

1. In a serving bowl, whisk together the vinegar, ginger, and canola oil.

2. Cook the ramen noodles in boiling water for 3 minutes, or according to the package directions (discard the ramen seasoning). Drain in a colander and rinse under cold water until cool. Add the noodles to the bowl with the dressing and toss with the cucumber and scallion to coat all the ingredients well with the dressing. Sprinkle with the sesame seeds. Serve immediately or chill in the refrigerator for several hours before serving.

. . . .

CHOPPED LOUIS SALAD

The Louis salad, whether made with crab or shrimp, has been a popular staple on West Coast menus since the early 1900s. This is a deliciously cool option for lunch or dinner. To dress it up, you can serve it inside avocado halves or in Bibb lettuce cups. Or try it as a side to a bowl of gazpacho. You can purchase cooked shrimp from the seafood counter at most grocery stores, or in the freezer case. Old Bay Seasoning can be found in the spice section of most supermarkets. If you can't find it, any type of spice blend appropriate for seafood would work. **Serves 2**

¼ cup mayonnaise

¼ cup sour cream

2 tablespoons ketchup

2 tablespoons sweet relish

1 tablespoon chopped flat-leaf parsley

1 package ramen noodles, shrimp flavor

2 tablespoons unsalted butter

1 teaspoon seafood seasoning, preferably Old Bay

½ head iceberg lettuce, finely sliced into 1-inch strips

½ cucumber, peeled and chopped

4 radishes, stemmed and thinly sliced

2 ribs celery, finely sliced

1 hard-boiled egg, chopped (see page 90)

½ avocado, diced

8 ounces cooked bay shrimp

6 cherry tomatoes, halved

1. In a small bowl, stir together the mayonnaise, sour cream, ketchup, relish, parsley, and 1 teaspoon of the ramen seasoning to combine (reserve the remainder). Cover and refrigerate until needed.

2. Preheat the oven to 350°F. In a small sauté pan, melt the butter over medium heat. Add the remaining ramen seasoning and the seafood seasoning, and stir to combine. Crush the ramen noodles, add to the pan, and stir to combine. Spread on a rimmed baking sheet and bake until browned, about 5 minutes. Remove from the oven and cool.

3. In a large bowl, combine the lettuce, cucumber, radishes, celery, egg, avocado, and cooled ramen. Divide the salad between two serving bowls. Top each salad with half of the bay shrimp and 6 tomato halves. Drizzle the dressing over each salad and serve.

● ● ● ● ● ● ● ● ●

HOW TO HARD-BOIL EGGS

Put the desired number of eggs in a saucepan and pour in enough water to cover the eggs by 1 inch. Over medium-high heat, bring the water just to a boil. Remove the pan from the heat, cover, and let stand for 12 minutes. Remove the eggs from the water and submerge them in a bowl of water, changing the water as needed if it warms up, until the eggs are cool to the touch. Eggs will keep in the refrigerator for up to one week.

SIDE DISHES

When I was growing up, my mother would often serve noodles of some sort as a side dish: macaroni and cheese, herbed noodles in a creamy sauce, or cold pasta salad. Somehow they went with everything, whether we were having fried chicken, steak, or broiled fish. A package of ramen noodles in the pantry and a few more ingredients means you can quickly and easily round out a dinner in a variety of ways. Like the noodle dishes that my mom used to rely on, the assortment of recipes in this chapter should be enough to accompany your main courses, whatever might be in the oven or on the stove.

RAMEN-N-CHEESE

This version of macaroni and cheese gives the impression of being lighter than the traditional dish by using the ramen noodles in place of macaroni. However, the cheese sauce packs a flavorful punch, incorporating the chicken seasoning to enrich the flavor. **Serves 4**

2 packages ramen noodles, chicken flavor

2½ tablespoons unsalted butter, divided

1 tablespoon all-purpose flour

½ teaspoon ground dry mustard

½ cup milk, divided

½ cup cream

1½ cups shredded sharp cheddar cheese (6 ounces)

1. Set aside half of 1 ramen noodle cake. Break the remaining 1½ noodle cakes into quarters and cook in boiling water for 3 minutes, or according to the package instructions (reserve 1 packet ramen seasoning, discard the other). Drain the noodles, reserving the cooking liquid.

2. Break the reserved ½ noodle cake into the bowl of a food processor and pulse until ground into a fine powder, the consistency of fine bread crumbs. In a small bowl in the microwave or in a small saucepan, melt ½ tablespoon butter. Off heat, add the ramen crumbs and stir to coat. If using a small saucepan, transfer the crumbs to a small bowl. Set aside.

3. In a small saucepan, melt the remaining 2 tablespoons butter over low heat. Whisk in the flour, and continue whisking for 1 minute. Add the reserved ramen seasoning and the dry mustard, and whisk to combine. Add ¼ cup milk and whisk continuously to combine. Add the remaining milk and the cream, and whisk to combine. Turn the heat up to medium-high and cook, whisking constantly, until the mixture begins to thicken, about 4 minutes. Turn the heat to low and whisk in the cheddar cheese, ¼ cup at a time, until combined. If the cheese sauce is too thick, add the reserved ramen noodle cooking liquid 1 tablespoon at a time. Add the cooked ramen and stir to combine.

4. Preheat the oven to 350°F. Coat the inside of a medium baking dish (8 or 9 inches square) with cooking spray. Spoon the ramen and cheese mixture into the dish and sprinkle with the ground ramen crumbs. Bake until the ramen crumbs are browned, about 15 minutes. Serve immediately.

● ● ● ● ● ● ● ●

GREEN BEANS WITH CRUNCHY SESAME RAMEN TOPPING

Dress up plain old green beans with this fun recipe. The inspiration is the classic green bean casserole found on many Thanksgiving tables, but this dish, preferably made with fresh green beans, has a crisper, lighter taste. You can use frozen green beans if you'd like, but try to avoid canned beans as their flavor and texture is not as good. This dish is excellent alongside a piece of grilled tuna. **Serves 2**

1 package ramen noodles, any flavor

1 tablespoon unsalted butter

2 teaspoons sesame oil, divided

2 teaspoons sugar

1 tablespoon sesame seeds

2 tablespoons canned French fried onions

8 ounces green beans, trimmed

salt and pepper

1. Crumble the ramen noodles into a small bowl (discard the ramen seasoning). In a medium nonstick skillet over medium heat, melt the butter and add 1 teaspoon sesame oil. Add the sugar and stir until the sugar melts and the mixture is a little syrupy. Add the crumbled ramen noodles and the sesame seeds and sauté, stirring frequently, until the noodles are browned and the sesame seeds are clumped together with the ramen bits, 6 to 8 minutes. Remove from the heat, stir in the onions, and set aside.

2. Pour water into a large saucepan to a depth of 1 or 2 inches and put a steamer insert into the pan if you have one. Bring the water to a simmer and add the green beans. Cook until the green beans are bright green and tender, 4 to 6 minutes. Remove from the heat, drain if necessary, and transfer to a serving bowl. Drizzle the beans with the remaining 1 teaspoon sesame oil and a pinch each of salt and pepper. Sprinkle with the ramen-sesame topping and serve hot or warm.

* * * * * * * *

WARM LEMON POPPY SEED SALAD

This side dish is summery and colorful, with cubes of bright red pepper and strands of dark and light green zucchini. It's delicious to serve with anything grilled, from fish to burgers. **Serves 4 to 6**

2 packages ramen noodles, any flavor

juice of 2 lemons

1 teaspoon Dijon mustard

1 tablespoon honey

pinch of salt

¼ cup vegetable oil

1 tablespoon poppy seeds

1 small zucchini, cut into ribbons with a vegetable peeler

1 small red bell pepper, diced

1. Cook the ramen noodles in boiling water for 3 minutes, or according to the package directions (discard the ramen seasoning).

2. While the ramen noodles cook, in a serving bowl, whisk together the lemon juice, mustard, honey, and salt until the mixture is smooth. Whisking continually, slowly drizzle in the vegetable oil to make a thick, creamy dressing. Stir in the poppy seeds.

3. When the ramen noodles are cooked, drain and add to the bowl with the dressing. Add the zucchini and red peppers and toss to coat. Serve warm.

. . . .

HERBY BUTTERED NOODLES AND PEAS

Sometimes simple is best, as in this comforting, buttery noodle dish that is delicious alongside an easy frozen or prepared food like a rotisserie chicken or fish sticks. Of course, it also pairs nicely with something a little more elaborate, like a pot roast or a pork loin.

Serves 2

1 package ramen noodles, any flavor

1 cup frozen peas

2 tablespoons unsalted butter, diced

2 tablespoons chopped fresh parsley

salt and pepper

1. Cook the ramen noodles and the peas in boiling water for 3 minutes (discard the ramen seasoning). Drain and return to the pot.

2. Immediately add the butter, tossing the noodles to coat completely. Sprinkle with the parsley and season to taste with salt and pepper. Serve immediately.

Variations:

Try a different fresh herb for an entirely different dish. Tarragon, thyme, or marjoram would all be delicious. Basil would be tasty, too, especially if you use olive oil in place of the butter.

· · · · · · · ·

CREAMED CORN AND POTATO CASSEROLE

Put together this satisfying casserole and pop it in the oven. As it cooks, you'll have just enough time to grill a steak or sauté some chicken breasts. **Serves 4**

1 large potato, peeled and diced into ¾-inch pieces

2 tablespoons unsalted butter, divided, plus more to prepare the pan

½ teaspoon dried thyme

1 package ramen noodles, chicken flavor

1 medium onion, diced

1 (14½-ounce) can creamed corn

2 tablespoons chopped fresh chives

salt and pepper

1. Preheat the oven to 375°F. Butter a small casserole dish. Fill a medium saucepan with salted water and bring to a boil over high heat. Add the potato pieces and boil until they are still firm but can be pierced easily with a fork, 5 to 7 minutes. Drain and set aside.

2. Crumble the ramen noodles into a small bowl (reserve the ramen seasoning). In a medium nonstick skillet over medium heat, melt 1 tablespoon butter. Sprinkle the ramen seasoning and the thyme into the pan. Add the crumbled ramen noodles and sauté, stirring frequently, until the ramen is toasted, about 5 minutes. Transfer the noodles to a small bowl.

3. Add the remaining 1 tablespoon butter to the pan and melt over medium-high heat. Add the onion and sauté, stirring occasionally, until the onion is translucent, about 5 minutes. Stir in the creamed corn, potatoes, and chives, and heat until warmed through, 3 to 4 minutes. Season to taste with salt and pepper. Stir about half of the toasted ramen into the corn mixture. Spoon the mixture into the prepared casserole dish, and sprinkle with the remaining ramen. Bake until bubbling, about 20 minutes. Serve hot.

* * * * * * * *

SPAETZLE-STYLE RAMEN NOODLES

I can't go to a German restaurant without ordering cheese spaetzle, a sautéed noodle dish that usually includes caramelized onions and Emmentaler cheese. Spaetzle is a pain to make at home; you basically drop a soft, batterlike dough into boiling water using a gadget that looks a bit like a cheese grater. But I've found that by using broken ramen noodles, you can at least replicate the taste of this dish, if not the exact texture. Serve this with grilled or sautéed sausages—preferably bratwurst—and a cold beer. **Serves 2 as a side dish or 1 as a main course**

1 teaspoon extra-virgin olive oil

1 medium onion, peeled, halved, and sliced

salt and pepper

1 package ramen noodles, any flavor

2 tablespoons unsalted butter

1/3 cup finely shredded Emmentaler cheese (about 1 ounce)

1 tablespoon chopped fresh parsley

1. In a small skillet, heat the olive oil over medium-low heat. Add the onion and cook, stirring occasionally, until brown and caramelized, about 20 minutes. Season with a pinch of salt, remove from the pan, and set aside.

2. While the onions are cooking, break the ramen noodles into about eight pieces and cook in boiling water for 2½ minutes (discard the ramen seasoning). Drain.

3. Melt the butter in the skillet over medium heat, add the ramen noodles, and sauté until they begin to brown, about 5 minutes. Stir in the onion and the cheese and cook, stirring, until the cheese melts, 3 to 4 minutes. Season to taste with salt and pepper, and stir in the parsley. Serve hot.

· · · · · · · · ·

STUFFED BAKED POTATOES WITH RAMEN ROMANO SPRINKLE

There's something so luscious about a perfectly baked potato: the fluffy interior mixed with butter and sour cream and generously seasoned with salt and pepper. This version is inspired by my memories of the stuffed-potato trend years ago, when baked-potato shops opened up in food courts and even some fast-food restaurants had stuffed baked potatoes on their menus. These potatoes are filled with broccoli and get a little extra crunch from Ramen Romano Sprinkle. **Serves 2**

2 large russet potatoes, scrubbed clean and patted dry

canola oil or vegetable oil

salt

½ cup chopped fresh or frozen broccoli

salt and pepper

2 tablespoons unsalted butter

¼ cup sour cream

2 tablespoons chopped fresh chives

2 tablespoons Ramen Romano Sprinkle (page 78)

1. Preheat the oven to 350°F. Using a fork, poke holes in the potatoes on all sides, about 8 times each. Rub the potatoes with oil and sprinkle them with kosher salt. When the oven is hot, put the potatoes directly on the rack (lay a sheet of aluminum foil on the rack beneath them to catch drips) and bake for 1 hour.

2. While the potatoes are cooking, pour water into a small saucepan to a depth of about 1 inch. Put a steamer insert in the pan if you have one. Bring the water to a simmer and add the broccoli. Steam the broccoli until it is bright green and can be pierced easily with a fork, 5 to 7 minutes. Season lightly with salt and pepper, set aside, and keep warm in the pan with the lid on.

3. When the potatoes are cooked, remove from the oven and let cool slightly. Make a cut lengthwise across the top of each potato and squeeze slightly to open it. Scoop out the flesh into a small bowl. Add the butter, sour cream, and chives, and mix with a fork, mashing the potato against the sides of the bowl to make it smooth. Season to taste with salt and pepper.

4. Spoon the seasoned potato filling back into the skins. Top with the steamed broccoli and sprinkle with the Ramen Romano Sprinkle. Serve immediately.

* * * * * * * *

RAMEN-BREADED ONION RINGS

Ramen makes a substantial, crunchy coating on onion rings, and the seasoning packet gives them a unique flavor. I like Vidalia onions for making onion rings because they're bigger than other onions, and they have a nice sweet taste that's even better after a few moments in the deep fryer. If you can't find roast chicken ramen noodles, regular chicken-flavored noodles are fine. **Serves 2 to 3**

2 packages ramen noodles, roast chicken flavor

1 cup all-purpose flour

salt

2 large eggs

1 Vidalia onion, cut into thick slices and separated into rings

vegetable or canola oil, for deep-frying

1. Break the ramen noodles into the bowl of a food processor and pulse until finely ground, resembling the consistency of bread crumbs. Transfer to a shallow bowl or pie plate and stir in the ramen seasoning.

2. In a second shallow bowl, mix together the flour and 1 teaspoon salt. In a third shallow bowl, lightly beat the eggs. Set up your breading station so that you can dip the onion rings first in the flour, next in the eggs, and finally in the ramen crumbs (for more information about breading, see Breading Tips and Tricks, page 107).

3. Working with one or two rings at a time, dredge the onions in the flour and dust off any excess. Then dip them in the egg, coating completely. Finally, dredge them in the ramen crumbs, pressing the crumbs against the inside and outside of each onion ring. Place the breaded onions on a rimmed baking sheet. Let sit for 20 to 30 minutes before cooking.

4. Line a rimmed baking sheet with paper towels. Pour oil into a large heavy-bottomed pot to a depth of 3 inches. Heat the oil over medium-high heat until the temperature is 350° to 375°F on a deep-frying thermometer, about 10 minutes. When the oil is ready, lower the heat to maintain the proper temperature.

5. Carefully drop the onion rings into the hot oil, adding only as many as will fit in the pot without crowding. Fry for about 40 seconds, then use a slotted spoon to gently turn the onion rings over and fry until golden brown, 30 to 40 seconds longer. Transfer the onion rings to the prepared baking sheet and sprinkle with salt. Repeat with the remaining onion rings. Serve immediately, while still hot.

* * * * * * * * *

BREADING TIPS AND TRICKS

Learning how to properly bread foods is an invaluable culinary skill. This method will enable you to make a wide range of breaded meat and vegetable dishes easily, efficiently, and with minimal mess.

Select your breading ingredients.
There are typically three components to breading:

Flour: Coating the food with flour (usually all-purpose flour) provides a uniformly dry surface. You can add a layer of flavor by seasoning the flour with salt, pepper, or finely powdered flavorings like paprika or cumin (or a ramen seasoning packet).

Egg: This element adds richness and provides a moist surface for the breading to stick to. The eggs should be beaten lightly with a fork or a whisk; you can add a little milk and water to thin it out.

Breading: The exterior breading is typically a dry, crunchy ingredient like bread crumbs, crushed crackers, or, as in many cases in this book, even crushed ramen noodles. For flavor, mix the breading with grated hard cheese like Parmesan, or fresh or dried herbs.

Arrange your breading station.
You can buy a set of breading trays—shallow rectangular trays that interlock to create a tidy setup—but it's not necessary. Pie pans are the ideal size and depth for breading. Arrange them closely together on rimmed baking sheets or a large cutting board to make cleanup easy. Your setup should be in this order, from left to right:

- The unbreaded food
- Flour
- Egg
- Breading
- Breaded food (arrange in a single layer on a tray or a rimmed baking sheet)

Breading tips:

- The food you are breading should be relatively thin, about ½ to ¾ inch thick. This will allow it to cook completely through without burning the exterior. Make sure that each piece is the same thickness so all the pieces will cook in the same amount of time.

- Be sure the food you are breading is as dry as possible before you dredge it in the flour. Pat it dry first with a paper towel.

- Use one of your hands to dip the foods in the flour, the other hand to dip it into the egg, and the first hand again to remove the breaded food from the breading pan. By using only one hand to work with the food when it's in the egg mixture, you will avoid getting your hand caked with flour and breading.

- Refrigerate the breaded food for 30 minutes to an hour before frying. This will help the breading set and will give you better frying results.

- Use enough oil when you fry. The pan should contain about ½ inch of oil, or enough to reach halfway up the piece of food.

- Make sure the oil is hot enough. When you put the food in the oil, it should immediately start sizzling. Test the hotness of the oil by dipping just a corner of the first piece of food in, and take it out if it doesn't sizzle.

A typical breading station (from left to right): unbreaded food, flour, eggs, breading, breaded food.

SESAME RAMEN NOODLES

Here's a basic, all-purpose noodle dish that's not meant to be eaten on its own. Instead, it's a subtly flavorful base for stir-fries, curries, sautéed vegetables, grilled meats, or any other dish you might otherwise serve on rice. It's an easy way to add another dimension of flavor and sophistication to a meal. **Serves 2**

1 package ramen noodles, any flavor

2 teaspoons sesame oil

1 tablespoon sesame seeds

1. Cook the ramen noodles in boiling water for 3 minutes, or according to the package directions (discard the ramen seasoning). Drain and return to the pot. Drizzle the noodles with the sesame oil and sprinkle with sesame seeds, and toss.

• • • • • • • • •

ASIAN-INSPIRED CLASSICS

Noodles are as endemic to Asian cuisine as they are to Italian fare—nearly every Asian country and region has at least one type of noodle dish. Take them out of their usual bowl of soup, and packaged ramen noodles are a nice element in a variety of Asian noodle dishes, both traditional and modern. What's more, a mound of chewy ramen noodles can be used much in the same way rice is used in Asian cooking: to soak up delicious flavors like Thai curry or the sweet-tart sauce that tops sesame chicken.

Use these recipes as a guide to incorporating ramen noodles into your favorite Asian dishes. And next time you're stir-frying vegetables, boil up a packet of ramen. Ready in just 3 minutes, they take far less time to prepare than a pot of rice!

COLD SESAME NOODLES

At once sweet, spicy, nutty, and cool, cold sesame noodles have always been one of my favorites on Chinese take-out menus. This is ideal picnic fare: The noodles will stay fresh for a few hours even if they're not refrigerated, and there's nothing in the dish that will spoil.

Serves 2

¼ cup smooth peanut butter

1 tablespoon plus 1 teaspoon rice vinegar

1 teaspoon soy sauce

1 teaspoon brown sugar

¼ teaspoon minced garlic

½ teaspoon grated fresh ginger

½ teaspoon sesame oil

1 package ramen noodles, any flavor

1 tablespoon sesame seeds, plus more for garnish

1 scallion, green and light green parts, thinly sliced

¼ cup diced peeled cucumber

1. In a small bowl, whisk together the peanut butter, rice vinegar, soy sauce, brown sugar, garlic, ginger, and sesame oil. Set aside.

2. Cook the ramen noodles in boiling water for 2½ minutes (discard the ramen seasoning). Drain in a colander then return the hot noodles immediately to the pot. Add the sauce and stir to coat completely. Stir in 1 tablespoon sesame seeds. To serve, place the noodles in a bowl and top with the scallions, cucumber, and additional sesame seeds. The noodles will keep, covered and refrigerated, for 2 to 3 days. If the noodles clump together, break them up a little with a fork before serving.

• • • • • • • • •

LOADED STIR-FRY

A good stir-fry recipe means you'll never go hungry, especially if there are miscellaneous vegetables and meats in your refrigerator or freezer. This basic recipe leaves plenty of room for adaptation: Use whatever vegetables you like, or are in season, or happen to be in your crisper; use the kind of meat or seafood you prefer; and adjust the ingredients in the sauce according to the flavors you like best. **Serves 2**

⅓ cup vegetable or chicken broth

2 tablespoons soy sauce

1 tablespoon rice cooking wine

1 tablespoon brown sugar

1 teaspoon sesame oil

1 teaspoon cornstarch

1 package ramen noodles, Oriental flavor

1 tablespoon vegetable oil

1 clove garlic, minced

1 teaspoon minced or grated fresh ginger

1 carrot, peeled and thinly sliced

½ onion, thinly sliced

½ cup packaged cabbage slaw mix

½ cup chopped green bell pepper

½ cup chopped red bell pepper

4 ounces tail-on shrimp, peeled and deveined

1. In a small bowl, whisk together the broth, soy sauce, rice cooking wine, brown sugar, sesame oil, cornstarch, and ramen seasoning. Whisk until the sugar and the cornstarch dissolve.

2. Break the ramen noodles into smaller pieces, if desired, then cook in boiling water for 3 minutes, or according to the package directions. Drain and set aside.

3. Heat the vegetable oil in a wok or a large nonstick skillet over high heat. Add the garlic and the ginger and cook, stirring constantly, for 30 seconds. Add the carrot, onion, and cabbage slaw mix and stir-fry for 2 to 3 minutes. Add the green and red bell pepper and the shrimp and stir-fry until the vegetables are crisp-tender and the shrimp are opaque and cooked through, about 5 minutes.

4. Whisk the sauce to recombine the ingredients and pour it over the mixture in the wok. Bring to a boil and simmer until the sauce is thickened and slightly glossy, about 2 minutes, stirring to coat all the ingredients. Stir in the cooked ramen noodles. Serve immediately.

Variations:

Other ingredients that would make great additions to a stir-fry are edamame, snow peas, shiitake mushrooms, broccoli, bok choy, tomato wedges, baby corn, water chestnuts, green beans, and scallions. Tofu, chicken, scallops, and beef are good alternatives for the protein.

. . . .

SESAME-CRUSTED TUNA WITH PONZU GLAZE ON RAMEN NOODLES

I made a version of this recipe for dinner the night I met my now-husband's parents. It was actually the perfect recipe for such an occasion—it's quick to prepare yet looks and tastes like something you'd get at a nice restaurant. To this day, it's still a recipe I bring out when I need to impress someone. **Serves 2**

¼ cup ponzu sauce or soy sauce

2 tablespoons honey

2 teaspoons sesame oil, divided

2 scallions, white and green parts, thinly sliced separately

2 (4-ounce) tuna steaks, about 1 inch thick

½ cup sesame seeds

2 teaspoons vegetable oil

1 package ramen noodles, any flavor

1. In a zip-top bag or a bowl, combine the ponzu or soy sauce, honey, 1 teaspoon sesame oil, and white part of the scallion. Add the tuna steaks and marinate for 5 minutes. Place sesame seeds on a plate or in a shallow bowl. Remove the tuna from the marinade, reserving the marinade, and press the tuna into the sesame seeds, turning to coat all sides.

2. Heat the vegetable oil in a small nonstick skillet over high heat. Add the tuna and cook until the exterior is browned but the interior is still red, 4 to 5 minutes, turning over halfway through cooking. Remove from the pan and keep warm on a plate covered loosely with aluminum foil. Add the marinade to the pan; it should immediately boil and thicken. Remove at once from the heat, stirring rapidly.

3. Cook the ramen noodles in boiling water for 3 minutes or according to the package directions (discard the ramen seasoning). Drain, return to the pot, and toss with the remaining 1 teaspoon sesame oil. Divide the noodles between two plates, thinly slice the tuna, and arrange the slices on the noodles. Drizzle with the glaze and garnish with the green parts of the scallion before serving.

· · · · · · · · ·

BEEF AND PEPPER BOWL

Simple, quick, and tasty, this is a great weeknight dish that can be made in less than 15 minutes. Use a combination of red, yellow, and green bell peppers for color. **Serves 2**

2 tablespoons rice vinegar

¼ cup soy sauce

1 tablespoon honey

½ teaspoon ground cumin

½ teaspoon cornstarch

1 teaspoon sesame oil

3 scallions, thinly sliced

8 ounces flank steak or hanger steak, trimmed of excess fat and thinly sliced into strips

1 package ramen noodles, any flavor

2 teaspoons vegetable or canola oil

1 bell pepper, any color, sliced

1. In a shallow bowl, whisk together the rice vinegar, soy sauce, honey, cumin, cornstarch, sesame oil, and scallions until the cornstarch dissolves. Add the beef and marinate for 5 minutes.

2. Meanwhile, cook the ramen noodles in boiling water for 3 minutes, or according to the package directions (discard the ramen seasoning). Drain and set aside.

3. Heat the oil in a medium nonstick skillet over medium-high heat. Use a fork or a slotted spoon to remove the meat from the marinade, reserving the marinade, and add the meat to the pan, along with the bell pepper. Sauté until the meat is cooked through, about 5 minutes. Add the noodles. Pour the reserved marinade over the noodle and meat mixture and cook until the marinade has thickened, about 1 to 2 minutes longer. Serve hot.

· · · · · · · · ·

TERIYAKI CHICKEN STIR-FRY

Bottled teriyaki sauce makes an easy shortcut for this dish, and canned pineapple gives it a little extra sweetness. Make it look restaurant quality by cutting the carrots and celery diagonally, the way Asian chefs do. **Serves 2**

1 tablespoon vegetable oil

2 carrots, peeled and sliced diagonally

2 ribs celery, sliced diagonally

1 small onion, cut into wedges

1 boneless, skinless chicken breast, sliced into ½-inch strips

¼ cup plus 1 tablespoon teriyaki sauce, divided

½ cup drained canned pineapple chunks

1 package ramen noodles, any flavor

1. In a large nonstick pan, heat the vegetable oil over medium-high heat. Add the carrots, celery, and onion, and stir-fry until the vegetables are crisp-tender, about 5 minutes.

2. In a large bowl, toss the chicken with 1 tablespoon teriyaki sauce. Add the chicken to the pan along with the pineapple. Stir-fry until the chicken is cooked through, 4 to 5 minutes. Stir in the remaining ¼ cup teriyaki sauce, stirring to coat. Cook until the sauce is heated through, about 2 minutes longer.

3. Cook the ramen noodles in boiling water for 3 minutes, or according to the package directions (discard the ramen seasoning).

4. Divide the cooked noodles between two bowls and top with equal parts of the teriyaki chicken mixture.

· · · · · · · · ·

SOY-EDAMAME RAMEN

This simple dish of noodles, edamame, and a tangy sauce makes for a quick, easy lunch or a satisfying side dish alongside an Asian-style fish recipe. **Serves 1**

½ cup frozen shelled edamame

1 package ramen noodles, Oriental or miso flavor

2 tablespoons soy sauce

1 tablespoon rice vinegar

½ teaspoon sesame oil

1. Bring a small pot of water to a boil over high heat. Add the edamame and simmer over medium-high heat for 3 minutes. Add the ramen noodles and simmer until the noodles are cooked, about 3 minutes longer (reserve the ramen seasoning).

2. While the edamame and ramen are cooking, in a small bowl, stir together the soy sauce, rice vinegar, sesame oil, and ramen seasoning.

3. Drain the noodles and edamame, return to the pot, and drizzle with the sauce. Serve warm.

· · · · · · · · ·

PAD THAI

This traditional Thai noodle dish is usually made with long, chewy rice noodles, but ramen noodles make a fine stand-in. You might be surprised to learn how few ingredients the sauce contains, considering it achieves such a complex-tasting balance of salty, sweet, sour, and spicy. Look for tamarind paste and fish sauce in the Asian section of your supermarket, and refrigerate what you don't use for this dish; both ingredients last for months. **Serves 2**

3 tablespoons tamarind paste

3 tablespoons fish sauce

¼ cup brown sugar

2 teaspoons soy sauce

½ teaspoon Thai chili sauce

1 package ramen noodles, any flavor

2 teaspoons vegetable oil

3 ounces baked tofu, Thai flavor

2 scallions, light green and white parts, thinly sliced

1 large egg

Garnishes:

2 tablespoons chopped peanuts

¼ cup mung beans

1 tablespoon chopped cilantro

2 lime wedges

1. In a small saucepan, combine the tamarind paste, fish sauce, and brown sugar. Bring to a simmer over medium-high heat and cook until thickened and the brown sugar is melted, about 5 minutes. Stir in the soy sauce and ½ teaspoon chili sauce or to taste. Remove from the heat and set aside.

2. Break the ramen noodles into 4 pieces and cook in boiling water for 3 minutes, or according to the package directions (discard the ramen seasoning). Drain.

3. Heat the vegetable oil over high heat. Add the noodles, tofu, and scallions, and stir-fry for 3 to 5 minutes. Reduce the heat to medium and break the egg into the pan. Stir the egg into the noodle mixture until the egg is scrambled, 45 seconds to 1 minute. Pour the sauce into the pan and cook until all of the ingredients are heated through, 2 to 3 minutes, stirring to combine all the ingredients.

4. To serve, transfer to a serving bowl. Garnish with the peanuts, mung beans, cilantro, and lime.

● ● ● ● ● ● ● ● ●

SESAME CHICKEN AND BROCCOLI

Sesame chicken is a Chinese-restaurant favorite—crisp chicken pieces in a sticky-sweet sauce. The chicken is traditionally fried, but since deep-frying can be messy and involved, I've adapted a version I saw in a magazine in which the chicken is coated in an egg white and cornstarch mixture and pan-fried. **Serves 2**

3 tablespoons honey

2 tablespoons soy sauce

1 teaspoon rice vinegar

3 tablespoons sesame seeds, divided

4 tablespoons vegetable or canola oil, divided

3 cups broccoli florets

2 scallions, white and green parts, minced separately

2 cloves garlic, minced

1 large egg white

2 tablespoons cornstarch

1 pound boneless, skinless chicken breasts or thighs, cut into 1-inch chunks

salt and pepper

1 package ramen noodles, any flavor

1 teaspoon sesame oil

1. In a small bowl, stir together the honey, soy sauce, rice vinegar, and 2 tablespoons sesame seeds. Set aside.

2. Heat 1 tablespoon oil in a large nonstick skillet over high heat. Sauté the broccoli and white and light green parts of the scallions until the broccoli is bright green and crisp-tender, about 5 minutes. Add the garlic and cook, stirring constantly, for 30 seconds. Transfer the vegetables to a bowl and cover loosely with aluminum foil to keep warm.

3. Reduce the heat to medium-high and add the remaining 3 tablespoons oil to the now-empty pan. In a medium bowl, whisk together the egg white and cornstarch. Season the chicken with salt and pepper, and add to the egg white mixture, stirring to coat the chicken completely. Using a fork or a slotted spoon, remove the chicken from the bowl, letting any excess egg white drip off, and transfer the chicken to the pan. Cook, turning occasionally, until light golden on all sides and cooked through, 5 to 8 minutes. Cut into a piece if necessary to check doneness; the chicken should not be pink, and its internal temperature should measure 165°F on a meat thermometer. Use a spoon to remove any excess oil from the pan, then add the vegetables back into the pan. Pour the sauce into the pan and stir to combine.

4. Meanwhile, cook the ramen noodles in boiling water for 3 minutes, or according to the package directions (discard the ramen seasoning). Drain and return to the pot. Drizzle with sesame oil and sprinkle with the remaining 1 tablespoon sesame seeds. To serve, divide the noodles between two plates or shallow bowls. Top with the chicken-broccoli mixture and garnish with the reserved dark green parts of the scallions.

· · · · · · · · ·

GREEN COCONUT CURRY SHRIMP BOWL

Coconut curry sauce can be so addictive you'll find yourself slurping up every drop, but a tangle of ramen noodles is the best way to soak it up. You can use red curry paste instead of green for a different flavor; many people think one curry is spicier than the other, but that's not really the case. According to Simply Asia Foods, which manufactures the Thai Kitchen product line, red curry paste has a more roasted flavor, while green curry paste typically has more cumin and an earthier taste.

Serves 2

2 teaspoons canola or vegetable oil

1 small onion, cut in half and sliced

1 small red or yellow bell pepper, sliced

1 (14-ounce) can coconut milk

½ to 2 tablespoons green or red curry paste

1 teaspoon brown sugar

lime juice

6 ounces cooked shrimp, peeled and deveined

½ cup frozen peas

1 package ramen noodles, any flavor

1 tablespoon chopped fresh cilantro

1. Heat the oil in a medium saucepan over medium-high heat. Add the onion and bell pepper and sauté until softened, about 5 minutes. Add the coconut milk and ½ tablespoon curry paste. Simmer for 5 minutes, then taste and add brown sugar, a squeeze of lime, and more curry paste as needed.

2. Add the shrimp and the frozen peas and simmer for 10 minutes, until the shrimp and peas are heated through and the sauce is thickened.

3. Meanwhile, cook the ramen noodles in boiling water for 3 minutes, or according to the package directions (discard the ramen seasoning). Drain. To serve, divide the noodles between two shallow bowls. Ladle the curry mixture over the noodles and garnish with the chopped cilantro.

· · · · · · · · ·

DAN DAN NOODLES

No two versions of this Sichuan noodle dish seem to be the same in terms of what ingredients they contain or how they're seasoned, but the one element that most share is Sichuan peppercorns. This spice, the dried berry husk from a type of ash tree, has an inimitable tingly spiciness. It was banned for nearly forty years by the U.S. government because of concern that it could spread a disease to American trees. The ban was lifted in 2005, and now it's not hard to find in Asian grocery stores or even in the Asian foods section of many well-stocked supermarkets. **Serves 2**

1 tablespoon Sichuan peppercorns, ground in a spice grinder or with a mortar and pestle

1 tablespoon smooth peanut butter

2 tablespoons plus 2 teaspoons soy sauce, divided

2 teaspoons chile oil

1 teaspoon brown sugar

2 teaspoons canola or vegetable oil

3 scallions, light green and white parts, thinly sliced separately

8 ounces ground pork

1 tablespoon grated fresh ginger

1 clove garlic, minced

1 teaspoon rice cooking wine or dry sherry

1 package ramen noodles, any flavor

¼ cup sliced peeled cucumber, cut into matchsticks

1. In a small bowl, stir together the peppercorns, peanut butter, 2 tablespoons soy sauce, chile oil, and brown sugar. Set aside.

2. Heat the oil in a large nonstick skillet over medium-high heat. Set aside 1 tablespoon light green scallions, then add the remaining scallions, pork, ginger, and garlic to the pan and cook, breaking the pork into small crumbles, until the meat is well-cooked, browned, and slightly crispy. Add the rice wine and the remaining 2 teaspoons soy sauce and cook, stirring frequently, until the mixture is nearly dry. Set aside.

3. Cook the ramen noodles in boiling water for 3 minutes, or according to the package directions (discard the ramen seasoning). Drain, transfer to a serving bowl, and toss with the reserved peppercorn sauce. Sprinkle with the cooked pork mixture and garnish with the reserved light green scallions and the cucumbers.

. . . .

BEEF AND SCALLION RAMEN

I love the way scallions taste when they're sautéed—a little cooking softens them and mellows the oniony flavor. This simple recipe has a light soy-lime sauce that goes well with the beef and scallions. It's a perfect topping for Sesame Ramen Noodles, or even just on plain ramen. **Serves 1**

¼ cup soy sauce

1 tablespoon lime juice

1 teaspoon sesame oil

4 ounces flank steak or skirt steak, thinly sliced

6 scallions, halved lengthwise and cut diagonally into 1-inch pieces

1 package ramen noodles, chili flavor, or prepared Sesame Ramen Noodles (page 108)

1 tablespoon vegetable oil

1 teaspoon cornstarch

1. In a small bowl, whisk together the soy sauce, lime juice, sesame oil, and ¼ teaspoon of the ramen seasoning (discard the remainder). Add the steak and the scallions and marinate for 5 minutes.

2. While the steak marinates, cook the ramen noodles in boiling water for 3 minutes, or according to the package directions. Drain and set aside.

3. Heat the oil in a skillet over medium-high heat. With a fork or a slotted spoon, remove the steak and the scallions from the marinade, reserving the marinade, and add the meat and the scallions to the pan. Cook, stirring frequently, until the steak is browned and the scallions are softened, 2 to 3 minutes. Whisk the cornstarch into the marinade and pour it into the pan. Bring to a boil and cook, stirring, until the sauce thickens slightly, about 1 minute. Serve on a bed of ramen noodles.

• • • • • • • • •

HOME-STYLE COMFORT FOODS

Ramen can stand in for other types of noodles in a wide range of recipes. The nice thing is that they cook in a fraction of the time of most other noodles, so it really speeds up the cooking process. Using the dry noodles ground up in place of bread crumbs makes them even more versatile, as in meat loaf and crusted chicken or fish recipes.

INDIVIDUAL TURKEY MEAT LOAVES WITH CRUNCHY RAMEN TOPPING

Everyone knows that the best part of meat loaf is the slightly crunchy, sticky-sweet ends. If you make individual meat loaves, nobody has to fight over who gets the two coveted end pieces. Plus, mini loaves will cook faster than one large loaf. If you don't have a food processor to grind the ramen noodles, you can put the dry noodles in a zip-top bag, lay the bag on a countertop or a table, and crush the noodles with a pan or rolling pin. The cooked meat loaves keep well in the refrigerator for 2 to 3 days, or in the freezer, wrapped tightly in plastic wrap, for up to 6 months. **Serves 4**

1 package ramen noodles, any flavor

½ medium onion, finely chopped

1 pound ground turkey

¼ cup ketchup

3 tablespoons teriyaki sauce, divided

1 teaspoon dried thyme

1 large egg

1. Preheat the oven to 350°F and line a 9 x 13-inch baking pan with aluminum foil and spray the foil with cooking spray. Break the ramen noodles into the bowl of a food processor and pulse to grind until they resemble rolled oats (discard the ramen seasoning).

2. Set aside 2 tablespoons ground ramen. In a large bowl, stir together the onion, turkey, the remaining ground ramen, ketchup, 1 tablespoon teriyaki sauce, and thyme. In a small bowl, whisk the egg lightly, then stir it into the turkey mixture. You can use your hands to make sure the mixture is thoroughly combined.

3. Form the turkey mixture into four loaves and put them on the prepared baking pan. Brush the loaves with the remaining 2 tablespoons teriyaki sauce and sprinkle them with the remaining 2 tablespoons ground ramen noodles. Bake until the meat loaves are cooked through and the tops are browned, 30 to 40 minutes. The internal temperature of the meat loaves should be 165°F on a meat thermometer.

* * * * * * * * *

BUTTERED PARMESAN NOODLES WITH PEAS AND CORN

Cheese, butter . . . comfort food at its best! Keep bags of frozen peas and corn—or other mixed veggies—in the freezer so that you can make this yummy, satisfying recipe when you need an indulgent little one-pot meal. My friend Jennifer B. shared this recipe, saying it was one of her go-to college meals. Her serving suggestion? Gobble straight from the pot! **Serves 1 to 2**

½ cup frozen peas

½ cup frozen corn

1 package ramen noodles, any flavor

1½ tablespoons unsalted butter

2 tablespoons grated Parmesan cheese

½ teaspoon garlic powder

1. Bring a small pot of water to a boil over high heat. Add the peas and the corn and simmer for 3 minutes. Add the noodles and simmer until the noodles are cooked, about 3 minutes longer (discard the ramen seasoning).

2. Drain the noodles and vegetables, transfer to a bowl, and immediately add the butter. Toss until the butter has melted completely. Add 2 tablespoons Parmesan cheese or to taste and the garlic powder, stirring to coat the noodle mixture completely. Serve immediately.

• • • • • • • •

RAMEN-CRUSTED CHICKEN FINGERS WITH HONEY MUSTARD SAUCE

Dry ramen noodles make a crunchy, flavorful topping for chicken pieces. Kids will like eating these as finger foods, dipped into the honey mustard, ketchup, or sweet and tangy barbecue sauce. You can also serve them as a chicken satay–style appetizer, on skewers and with peanut sauce for dipping, or you can use them to top a green salad.

Serves 4

1 package ramen noodles, chicken flavor

⅛ cup yellow mustard

⅛ cup honey

1 pound boneless, skinless chicken breast or chicken cutlets, cut into strips

1. Preheat the oven to 400°F and line a rimmed baking sheet with parchment paper. Break the ramen noodles into the bowl of a food processor and pulse until the noodles are ground into small pieces, about the consistency of rolled oats. Transfer to a shallow bowl and mix with the ramen seasoning.

2. In a small bowl, stir together the mustard and honey. Spoon 1 to 2 tablespoons honey mustard into a second shallow bowl and reserve the rest for a dipping sauce.

3. Pat the chicken pieces dry and brush them with the honey mustard, then roll each piece in the ramen mixture, making sure to coat the chicken completely. Transfer the chicken pieces to the prepared baking sheet. Spray the chicken lightly with cooking spray and bake for 10 minutes. Turn the chicken pieces over, spray lightly with the cooking spray again, and bake until the chicken is cooked through, 5 to 10 minutes longer. If you cut into a piece of chicken, it should not be pink, and its internal temperature should measure 165°F on a meat thermometer. Serve with the remaining honey mustard sauce or barbecue sauce.

· · · · · · · · ·

RAMEN BOLOGNESE

Sometimes a little red-sauce pasta is just what you need, and a package of ramen noodles is the perfect amount for two (or for one healthy appetite). Set out a red-checkered tablecloth and a bottle of Chianti, and toast some garlic bread for a delicious Italian-style supper, just like Nonna used to make. Just don't tell her you used ramen noodles in place of Italian spaghetti! **Serves 2**

1 tablespoon extra-virgin olive oil

1 small onion, diced

1 clove garlic, minced

4 ounces ground turkey or ground beef

1 (15-ounce) can crushed tomatoes

1 tablespoon tomato paste

1 tablespoon dried Italian herbs

salt and pepper

1 package ramen noodles, any flavor

grated Parmesan cheese, for serving

1. In a medium saucepan, heat the olive oil over medium-high heat. Add the onion and sauté, stirring occasionally, until translucent and softened, about 5 minutes. Add the garlic and cook, stirring constantly, for 30 seconds. Add the beef or turkey and cook, breaking up the large chunks, until the meat is browned and cooked through, 5 to 7 minutes. Tilt the pan and use a spoon to remove excess oil or cooking liquid.

2. Stir in the tomatoes, tomato paste, and Italian herbs. Bring to a boil, then reduce the heat and simmer for 10 minutes to allow the flavors to meld. Season to taste with salt and pepper.

3. While the sauce is simmering, cook the ramen noodles in boiling water for 3 minutes, or according to the package directions (discard the ramen seasoning). Drain the noodles. To serve, divide the noodles between two bowls and top with Bolognese sauce. Sprinkle with Parmesan cheese.

• • • • • • • • •

BEEF STROGANOFF ON BUTTERED PARSLEY RAMEN NOODLES

Classic beef stroganoff is surprisingly quick and easy to make and has such a rich, creamy, satisfying flavor. The fresh parsley gives this dish a fresh, bright contrast to the creaminess of the sauce and adds a bit of color. **Serves 2**

1 tablespoon plus 1 teaspoon unsalted butter

1 shallot or ½ small onion, minced

½ cup sliced cremini mushrooms (5 ounces)

8 ounces flank steak or hanger steak, cut into thin strips

salt and pepper

¼ cup low-fat sour cream

1 package ramen noodles, any flavor

1 teaspoon butter

1 tablespoon chopped fresh parsley, plus more for garnish

1. In a medium nonstick skillet, melt the butter over medium heat. When the butter begins to foam, add the shallot or onion and cook until softened and translucent, 2 to 3 minutes. Add the mushrooms and cook until softened, stirring occasionally, 3 to 4 minutes. Season the steak with salt and pepper and add it to the pan. Cook on medium-high heat until cooked through, stirring and turning over the pieces, 3 to 4 minutes. Reduce the heat to medium-low and stir in the sour cream. Season to taste with salt and pepper.

2. While you're cooking the steak, cook the ramen noodles in boiling water for 3 minutes, or according to the package directions (discard the ramen seasoning). Drain, return to the pot, and add the butter and parsley.

3. To serve, divide the noodles between two plates or shallow bowls and top with the steak and mushroom mixture. Garnish with more parsley.

• • • • • • • •

BASIL PESTO NOODLES WITH CHICKEN

In the summer, use the bountifully available fresh basil to make up a batch of pungent pesto. It goes so perfectly with firm, thin ramen noodles. Add a grilled or sautéed chicken breast and it's the perfect summertime supper. A small, prep-size food processor is the perfect size to make this pesto recipe for two. Any extra sauce can be used as a spread on a turkey sandwich. **Serves 2**

1 clove garlic, minced

2 tablespoons pine nuts, toasted

¾ cup fresh basil leaves

3 tablespoons extra-virgin olive oil

½ cup grated Parmesan cheese

salt and pepper

2 (6-ounce) boneless, skinless chicken breasts, trimmed of excess fat

1 tablespoon vegetable oil

1 package ramen noodles, chicken flavor

1. In a food processor or blender, pulse the garlic and the pine nuts several times until the nuts are finely ground. Add the basil and pulse until the leaves are finely chopped, stopping to scrape the sides of the bowl as needed. With the motor running, drizzle in the olive oil until the mixture makes a loose paste.

2. Transfer the mixture to a small bowl and stir in the Parmesan cheese. Season to taste with salt and pepper. Cover by pressing plastic wrap against the surface of the pesto to keep it from browning, and set aside.

3. Place the chicken breasts between two pieces of plastic wrap and use a meat mallet or a rolling pin to pound them to an even thickness, about ¾-inch. Heat the vegetable oil in a small skillet or coat a grill pan with the oil and heat the pan over medium-high heat. Sprinkle the chicken breasts with the ramen seasoning on both sides. Add the breasts to the pan, smooth side down. Cook until browned and cooked through, 5 to 6 minutes on each side.

4. While the chicken is cooking, cook the ramen noodles in boiling water for 3 minutes, or according to the package directions. Drain and return to the pot. Add enough of the pesto to the hot noodles to generously coat evenly.

5. To serve, divide the noodles between two plates. Slice the chicken into strips, if desired, and arrange on the noodles.

＊＊＊＊＊＊＊＊

CILANTRO PESTO NOODLES

The bracing flavor of cilantro is toned down when it's combined with the traditional ingredients in pesto: Parmesan cheese, olive oil, and garlic. Press a piece of plastic wrap against the surface of any leftover pesto to keep it from turning brown, and store it in the refrigerator for a day or two. It's delicious stirred into scrambled eggs, as a sandwich spread, or on top of a piece of grilled chicken or fish. **Serves 2**

2½ cups fresh cilantro (from 1 large bunch)

1 clove garlic, coarsely chopped

¼ cup grated Parmesan cheese

½ cup chopped walnuts

¼ cup extra-virgin olive oil

lime juice

salt and pepper

1 package ramen noodles, any flavor

1. In a food processor, pulse the cilantro and garlic. Add the Parmesan cheese and the walnuts and pulse to puree to combine the ingredients well, stopping to scrape down the sides every so often. With the motor running, slowly drizzle in the olive oil through the feed tube until the mixture makes a loose paste.

2. Transfer the mixture to a small bowl and season to taste with lime juice, salt, and pepper. Cover by pressing plastic wrap against the surface of the pesto to keep it from browning, and set aside.

3. Cook the ramen noodles in boiling water for 3 minutes, or according to the package directions (discard the ramen seasoning). Drain the noodles, return to the pot, and toss with several generous spoonfuls of the pesto to coat well while still hot.

• • • • • • • • •

RAMEN ALFREDO WITH ASPARAGUS

Decadent Alfredo sauce is a wonderful indulgence. I love the way the sauce clings to skinny ramen noodles, and a handful of asparagus can cut the richness a little. **Serves 2**

1 cup heavy cream

4 tablespoons unsalted butter, cut into pieces

½ cup Parmesan cheese, plus more for serving

½ teaspoon garlic powder

pinch of nutmeg

black pepper

1 package ramen noodles, any flavor

1 cup chopped fresh or frozen asparagus (1-inch pieces)

1. In a medium saucepan, heat the cream to a simmer over medium heat. Add the butter and stir occasionally until completely melted. Add the cheese, garlic powder, and nutmeg. Simmer over medium-low heat, stirring frequently, until the cheese is melted and the mixture is smooth and creamy, about 5 minutes. Season to taste with pepper.

2. Meanwhile, cook the ramen noodles and asparagus for 3 minutes in boiling water (discard the ramen seasoning). Drain and return to the pot. Stir in the sauce to coat the noodles completely. To serve, divide the noodles between two bowls and sprinkle with additional Parmesan cheese.

Variation:

- Omit the asparagus. Mix the noodles with the sauce and top each serving with ½ cup sautéed wild mushrooms.

• • • • • • • • •

CHICKEN POTPIE

Classic comfort food, with a twist. Ground ramen noodles add texture to the pastry crust, while the chicken seasoning packet is just the right combination of flavors for the filling. This recipe is an ideal way to use up extra chicken or turkey from another meal, or you can purchase a rotisserie chicken for the meat. If you're starting out with uncooked meat, see How to Poach Chicken (page 84); use the meat and the broth for making the potpie. **Serves 4**

1 package ramen noodles, chicken flavor

½ cup plus 2 tablespoons all-purpose flour

salt and pepper

2 tablespoons unsalted butter, cut into small cubes

1 tablespoon minced fresh parsley

5 tablespoons ice water

2 tablespoons vegetable oil

1 small onion, chopped

2 ribs celery, chopped

2 carrots, peeled and chopped

1 large clove garlic, minced

3 cups chicken broth

1 pound cooked chicken meat, shredded

1 bay leaf

1. Preheat the oven to 350°F. Spray a 9-inch square pan with cooking spray. Break the ramen noodles into the bowl of a food processor (reserve the ramen seasoning) and pulse until they resemble fine bread crumbs. Measure out ½ cup ground ramen into a medium bowl. Discard the remaining ramen or use it for another recipe.

2. Add ½ cup flour and ½ teaspoon salt to the ramen and stir to combine. Add the butter to the bowl. Using two knives or a pastry cutter, cut the butter into the ramen and flour mixture until it is about the size of small peas. Add the parsley and stir to combine. Add 2 tablespoons ice water and stir with a spoon or your hands. Add the remaining 3 tablespoons water and continue to combine, until the dough just comes together (the dough will be sticky). Set aside.

3. Heat the vegetable oil in a large saucepan over medium-high heat. Add the onion, celery, and carrots, and sauté, stirring occasionally, until the onion is translucent, 4 to 5 minutes. Add the garlic and cook, stirring constantly, about 30 seconds. Stir in the chicken seasoning packet and the remaining 2 tablespoons flour. Cook for 1 minute, stirring constantly. Gradually stir in the chicken broth and bring to a simmer. Cook, stirring occasionally, until the broth begins to thicken, 4 to 5 minutes. Season to taste with salt and pepper, and add the chicken and the bay leaf. Pour the mixture into the prepared pan.

4. Lightly flour a cutting board. Flatten the dough using the palm of your hand. Using a rolling pin, roll out the dough to approximately ¼ inch thick. Lay the dough over the top of the chicken mixture in the pan and trim off any excess. Using a fork, poke the dough with several air holes.

5. Bake until the crust is browned and the filling is bubbling, about 30 minutes. Cover the dough with foil if the crust begins to brown too quickly. Remove from the oven and cool for 5 minutes before serving.

· · · · · · · · ·

RAMEN-CRUSTED TROUT

This trout recipe makes for a great 30-minute meal but is so delicious you can serve it to a guest and they will think you spent hours preparing for their arrival. Complete the feast with wild rice and roasted asparagus. **Serves 2**

2 trout fillets

salt and pepper

1 package ramen noodles, Oriental flavor

⅓ cup all-purpose flour

1 large egg

1 tablespoon extra-virgin olive oil

3 tablespoons unsalted butter, divided

1 shallot, minced

⅓ cup dry white wine

1. Season both sides of the trout fillets with salt and pepper.

2. Break the ramen noodles into the bowl of a food processor, add the ramen seasoning, and pulse to grind until they resemble fine bread crumbs. Transfer to a shallow bowl or a pie plate. In a second shallow bowl, place the flour. In a third shallow bowl, beat the egg. Line a plate with paper towels.

3. In a large skillet, heat the olive oil and 1 tablespoon butter over medium-high heat until the butter melts, tilting the pan to coat the bottom completely with the oil and butter. Bread the trout fillets by coating both sides of each fillet first in flour, then in egg, then in the ramen mixture (See Breading Tips and Tricks, page 106, for more detailed instructions on breading). Put the trout fillets immediately in the hot skillet and cook on one side until browned, about 2 minutes, then flip the fillets over and cook 2 minutes longer. Transfer the cooked trout fillets to the prepared plate.

4. Add the shallot to the skillet and cook, stirring constantly, until translucent, about 1 minute. Add the wine and bring to a simmer. Cook until the liquid is reduced by half, 3 to 4 minutes. Reduce the heat to low and whisk in the remaining 2 tablespoons butter. Remove from the heat and season to taste with salt and pepper.

5. To serve, plate each trout fillet and spoon half of the wine sauce over each one.

· · · · · · · · ·

MEATLESS MEALS

Ramen noodles make a versatile and tasty base for meatless recipes of all kinds. If you're a vegetarian, just make sure to check the ingredient list on the ramen brand you buy—many of the seasoning packets contain meat products. In addition to the recipes in this chapter, there are plenty of other recipes throughout this book that don't contain meat or could be adapted to be meatless.

QUICK VEGGIE STIR-FRY

You can find packages of frozen stir-fry vegetables in the freezer aisle of pretty much any supermarket. The vegetable combinations in these packages vary, so find one that has all your favorites and keep a bag on hand so that you'll always be able to make this satisfying dinner.

Serves 1

1 package ramen noodles, mushroom or miso flavor

2 tablespoons soy sauce

½ teaspoon sesame oil

1 teaspoon vegetable oil

1½ cups frozen mixed stir-fry vegetables

1 teaspoon chopped fresh or jarred ginger

1 clove garlic, minced

1 large egg

1 tablespoon sesame seeds, for garnish (optional)

1. Cook the ramen noodles in boiling water for 3 minutes, or according to the package directions (reserve the ramen seasoning). Drain and return to the pot to keep warm, covered, until needed. In a small bowl, whisk together 1½ teaspoons ramen seasoning (discard the remainder), soy sauce, and sesame oil. Set aside.

2. Meanwhile, heat the vegetable oil in a large nonstick skillet over high heat, tilting the pan to coat it with the oil. Add the vegetables and cook, stirring frequently, for 4 to 5 minutes. Reduce the heat to medium and add the ginger and garlic. Cook, stirring constantly, for 30 seconds.

3. Add the noodles and the soy sauce mixture to the pan and stir, using the edge of a spatula to cut the noodles into smaller pieces. Stir-fry for 2 to 3 minutes. Break the egg into the middle of the pan and immediately begin stirring and breaking up the egg with the spatula until the egg is cooked through, 30 to 45 seconds.

4. Serve hot, sprinkled with sesame seeds if desired.

· · · · · · · · ·

RAMEN WITH CHERRY TOMATOES AND MOZZARELLA

This quick pasta dish has a no-cook sauce that's particularly tasty in the summer when tomatoes are at their best. My favorite part about this sauce is how the heat from the pasta melts the mozzarella a little.

Serves 2

1 cup cherry tomatoes, quartered

1 tablespoon chopped kalamata olives

2 tablespoons chopped fresh basil

4 ounces fresh mozzarella, diced

2 tablespoons extra-virgin olive oil

salt and pepper

1 package ramen noodles, any flavor

2 tablespoons grated Parmesan cheese

1. In a medium bowl, combine the tomatoes, olives, basil, and mozzarella. Drizzle with the olive oil and stir to combine. Season to taste with the salt and pepper.

2. Cook the ramen noodles in boiling water for 3 minutes, or according to the package directions (discard the ramen seasoning). Drain and return to the pot. Immediately add the tomato mixture and stir to combine. Divide the mixture between two plates or shallow bowls and sprinkle with the Parmesan cheese.

• • • • • • • •

SESAME-CRUSTED TOFU ON GINGER-LIME NOODLES

I love the crunch that sesame gives when it's used as a crust for tofu, which has such a soft, yielding texture. Hoisin sauce makes the seeds stick and gives a hint of sweetness, which is nicely offset by the tangy noodles. **Serves 2**

juice of 1 lime

2 tablespoons soy sauce

1 teaspoon grated fresh ginger

3 tablespoons vegetable oil, divided

1 (14-ounce) block extra-firm tofu, halved horizontally

½ cup sesame seeds

1 tablespoon hoisin sauce

½ cup frozen shelled edamame

1 package ramen noodles, any flavor

2 scallions, green part only, thinly sliced

1. In a small bowl, whisk together the lime juice, soy sauce, ginger, and 1 tablespoon vegetable oil. Set aside.

2. Pat the tofu dry with a paper towel. Place the sesame seeds on a shallow plate. Brush all sides of the tofu with hoisin sauce, then press the tofu into the sesame seeds, turning to coat the block of tofu completely.

3. Heat the remaining 2 tablespoons vegetable oil in a nonstick skillet over medium-high heat. When the oil is hot, add the tofu to the pan. Cook, undisturbed, until the sesame seeds form a browned crust, about 5 minutes. Turn the tofu over and cook 5 minutes longer. Be careful not to let the sesame seeds burn.

4. Meanwhile, bring a small pot of water to boil over high heat. Add the edamame and simmer for 2 minutes. Add the ramen noodles and cook for 3 minutes longer (discard the ramen seasoning). Drain and return to the pot. Whisk the lime–soy sauce again to recombine the ingredients and drizzle it over the noodles and edamame, tossing with a fork to combine.

5. To serve, divide the noodles between two plates. Slice each tofu piece in half diagonally and arrange them on the noodles with one piece diagonally leaning against the other. Garnish with the scallions.

* * * * * * * *

SPICY BASIL STIR-FRY

The sauce in this recipe has such complexity—spicy, sweet, garlicky—you'd never believe that it's really only a few ingredients. This dish can be made in less than 15 minutes and makes a satisfying one-pot meal.

Serves 2

¼ cup black bean garlic sauce

2 tablespoons Thai chili sauce

juice of ½ lime

1 tablespoon soy sauce

2 teaspoons brown sugar

1 package ramen noodles, any flavor

1 tablespoon vegetable oil

8 ounces extra-firm tofu, cut into 1-inch cubes

½ medium onion, cut in half and sliced

¾ cup bite-size broccoli florets

½ cup fresh whole basil leaves

1. In a small bowl, stir together the garlic sauce, chili sauce, lime juice, soy sauce, and brown sugar. Set aside.

2. Cook the ramen noodles in boiling water for 3 minutes, or according to the package directions (discard the ramen seasoning). Drain and set aside.

3. In a large wok or nonstick skillet, heat the vegetable oil over high heat. Add the tofu, onion, and broccoli and stir-fry until the tofu is lightly browned, the onion is soft, and the broccoli is bright green and crisp-tender, 5 to 7 minutes. Add the sauce and the basil and cook, stirring, until all the ingredients are coated and the basil is wilted, 1 to 2 minutes. Stir the noodles into the vegetables and serve immediately.

· · · · · · · · ·

ZUCCHINI BOATS FILLED WITH RAMEN AND MUSHROOMS

Roasted zucchini stuffed with a tasty filling never fails to impress. In this recipe, the filling is a mixture of sautéed mushrooms, meatless crumbles, and ramen noodles, all smothered with gooey melted mozzarella cheese. Kids especially love these "boats" and how the zucchini makes a bowl of sorts for the hearty filling. **Serves 4 as a main course or 8 as a side dish**

4 small zucchini

1 package ramen noodles, any flavor

2 teaspoons extra-virgin olive oil

½ cup diced onion

4 ounces cremini mushrooms, sliced

½ teaspoon dried Italian herbs or dried oregano

½ teaspoon ground cumin

salt and pepper

½ cup frozen meatless crumbles, like MorningStar Farms

¾ cup canned chopped tomatoes

1 cup shredded mozzarella cheese (4 ounces)

1. Preheat the oven to 375°F. Line a rimmed baking sheet with parchment paper. Cut the stems off the zucchini and cut them in half lengthwise. Hollow out each half by scooping out the seeds and some of the flesh. Put the zucchini cut side down on the prepared baking sheet and bake until slightly softened, about 15 minutes. Remove from the oven and turn the zucchini over so the hollow side is facing up. Preheat the broiler.

2. While the zucchini bakes, cook the ramen noodles in boiling water for 3 minutes, or according to the package directions (discard the ramen seasoning). Drain and set aside.

3. Heat the olive oil in a large nonstick skillet over medium-high heat. Add the onion and sauté until translucent, about 3 to 4 minutes. Add the mushrooms and cook until soft, 7 to 9 minutes. Add the herbs and the cumin, and season to taste with salt and pepper.

4. Add the meatless crumbles and cook until heated through. Stir in the noodles and tomatoes, and cook, stirring occasionally, until the mixture is heated, 4 to 5 minutes.

5. Divide the filling between the zucchini boats. Sprinkle evenly with cheese and broil until the cheese melts, about 3 minutes.

• • • • • • • • •

SEARED TOFU AND VEGGIE NOODLE BOWL

For tofu to get a chewy, golden exterior and creamy interior, you can't rush things. Just keep an eye on it sizzling in the pan and eventually your patience will be rewarded. For the best texture, be sure to buy extra-firm tofu; you can even press the sliced tofu under a weighted plate for 20 minutes to press out excess water and make it even firmer. A bag of frozen mixed stir-fry vegetables makes this dish quick and easy to prepare, but you can also use any combination of your favorite fresh vegetables. **Serves 2**

1 (14-ounce) block extra-firm tofu, cut in half lengthwise

1 tablespoon sesame oil

1 tablespoon vegetable oil

¼ cup plus 1 teaspoon soy sauce, divided

1 package ramen noodles, any flavor

2½ cups frozen stir-fry vegetable blend

2 tablespoons rice vinegar

½ teaspoon cornstarch

1. Pat the tofu dry on all sides with a paper towel, then brush two sides with sesame oil. Heat the vegetable oil in a large nonstick skillet over high heat. When the oil is hot, add the tofu. Cook on one side without disturbing until browned, about 7 minutes. Turn the tofu over and cook on the second side until browned, about 7 minutes longer. Transfer to a plate, drizzle with about 1 teaspoon soy sauce, and set aside.

2. While the tofu browns, cook the ramen noodles in boiling water for 3 minutes, or according to the package directions (discard the ramen seasoning). Drain and set aside.

3. Add the frozen vegetables to the skillet and cook on high heat, stirring frequently, until crisp-tender, 4 to 6 minutes. Add the cooked ramen noodles and stir to combine. In a small bowl, whisk together the remaining ¼ cup soy sauce, rice vinegar, and cornstarch. Drizzle the soy sauce mixture over the vegetables and noodles and cook until the sauce is thickened, 2 to 3 minutes. To serve, divide the vegetable-noodle mixture between two plates or noodle bowls and top each with one piece of seared tofu.

· · · · · · · · ·

STIR-FRIED VEGETABLES IN COCONUT-GINGER SAUCE

Ramen noodles soak up the delicate, subtly sweet coconut sauce in this surprisingly simple recipe. Use a package of frozen stir-fry vegetables or any combination of your favorite fresh or frozen veggies. **Serves 2**

1 tablespoon vegetable or canola oil

2 cups frozen stir-fry vegetables

1 clove garlic, minced

1 teaspoon minced ginger

¾ cup coconut milk

juice of 1 lime

1 teaspoon soy sauce

pinch of red pepper flakes

1 package ramen noodles, any flavor

1. Heat the oil in a large nonstick skillet. When the oil is hot, add the vegetables and cook, stirring frequently, until the vegetables are crisp-tender, about 5 to 7 minutes. Add the garlic and ginger and cook, stirring constantly, for 30 seconds. Add the coconut milk and simmer over medium-high heat, stirring occasionally, until the sauce is slightly thickened, 5 to 7 minutes. Season to taste with the lime juice, soy sauce, and red pepper flakes.

2. While the vegetables are cooking, cook the ramen noodles in boiling water for 3 minutes, or according to the package directions (discard the ramen seasoning). Drain.

3. Serve the vegetable mixture over the cooked ramen noodles or stir the noodles into the vegetable mixture in the pan.

RAMEN-CRUSTED EGGPLANT PARMESAN

This Italian classic is even better when ground dry ramen noodles are used to bread the eggplant before it's fried. Cooked in a casserole dish, layered with noodles and cheese, it makes a satisfying weeknight dinner when paired with a baguette and a green salad. Leftovers reheat nicely for lunch the next day. See "Breading Tips and Tricks" (page 106) for details on how to bread the eggplant. **Serves 4**

1 medium eggplant, cut crosswise into ½-inch slices

kosher salt

1 tablespoon extra-virgin olive oil

1 medium onion, chopped

1 clove garlic, minced

1 (28-ounce) can crushed tomatoes

2 tablespoons tomato paste

3 teaspoons dried Italian herbs or dried oregano, divided

2 packages ramen noodles, any flavor, divided

½ cup all-purpose flour

2 large eggs, lightly beaten

canola or vegetable oil, for frying

¾ cup shredded mozzarella cheese (3 ounces)

2 tablespoons grated Parmesan cheese

1. Sprinkle both sides of the eggplant slices with salt and place the slices in a colander in the sink. Let sit 20 minutes to extract any bitter flavors from the eggplant.

2. Meanwhile, make the tomato sauce. In a medium saucepan, heat the olive oil over medium-high heat. Add the onion and sauté, stirring occasionally, until the onion is softened and translucent, 4 to 5 minutes. Add the garlic and cook, stirring constantly, for 30 seconds. Add the tomatoes and tomato paste. Bring to a simmer, reduce the heat to medium-low, and simmer until the sauce has thickened slightly and the flavors have had a chance to combine, 5 to 10 minutes. Stir in 1 teaspoon herbs and season to taste with salt. Set aside.

3. Cook 1 package ramen noodles in boiling water for 3 minutes, or according to the package directions (discard the ramen seasoning). Drain and set aside.

4. Preheat the oven to 375°F. Line a plate with paper towels. Rinse the eggplant slices and pat dry with paper towels. Break the remaining package of ramen noodles into the bowl of a food processor and pulse to grind until they resemble rolled oats (discard the ramen seasoning). Transfer the ground noodles to a shallow bowl or pie plate and stir in the remaining 2 teaspoons herbs and a pinch of salt. Place the flour in a second shallow bowl. In a third shallow bowl, beat the eggs.

5. Put enough oil in a large nonstick skillet to cover the bottom by about a ½ inch. Heat the oil over medium-high heat until it shimmers. Bread the eggplant slices by coating both sides first in flour, then in egg, then in the ground noodle mixture. Put the eggplant slices immediately in the hot oil and fry on one side until browned, about 7 minutes, then flip the slices over and fry 7 minutes longer. Transfer the cooked eggplant to a paper towel–covered plate.

6. To assemble the eggplant parmesan, spread about ½ cup tomato sauce in the bottom of a casserole dish about 11 x 7 inches. Spread the cooked ramen noodles over the sauce. Arrange the fried eggplant slices on top of the noodles in a single layer, or slightly overlap them. Spread the remaining sauce over the eggplant, and sprinkle evenly with mozzarella and Parmesan cheese. Bake until the sauce is bubbling and the cheese is melted, about 20 minutes.

* * * * * * * *

KALE-CHEDDAR NOODLE CASSEROLE

This riff on macaroni and cheese includes kale, a hearty green that's supernutritious and has a nice bite to it. You can also use spinach, mustard greens, or any other leafy green. Kale often is available chopped and prewashed in a bag, which makes putting together this baked dish even easier. **Serves 4**

2½ cups chopped kale (about 1 bunch)

2½ packages ramen noodles, any flavor, divided

2 tablespoons unsalted butter, divided

¼ teaspoon garlic powder, plus more for topping, divided

2 tablespoons grated Parmesan cheese

1 tablespoon all-purpose flour

1 cup milk

½ teaspoon Dijon mustard

1 cup shredded cheddar cheese (4 ounces)

½ teaspoon salt

1. Preheat the oven to 350°F. Butter the bottom and sides of a small baking dish (about 8 inches square). Bring a medium pot of water to a boil over high heat. Add the kale and boil for 3 minutes. Add 2 packages ramen noodles and boil 3 minutes longer (discard the ramen seasoning). Drain the noodles and kale, return to the pot, and cover with a lid to keep warm.

2. To make the crunchy ramen topping, break the remaining ½-package ramen noodles into the bowl of a food processor and pulse to grind until they resemble rolled oats (discard the ramen seasoning). Transfer the ground noodles to a small bowl.

Melt 1 tablespoon butter in the microwave and add it to the dry noodles, as well as a pinch of garlic powder and the Parmesan cheese. Stir to combine and set aside.

3. In a medium saucepan, melt the remaining 1 tablespoon butter. Whisk in the flour and cook for 1 minute, until the mixture forms a clumpy paste. Gradually whisk in the milk, whisking after each addition until the mixture is smooth, to avoid lumps. When all the milk is incorporated, simmer, whisking frequently, until the mixture is thick and creamy, about 7 minutes. Stir in the mustard, cheese, salt, and remaining $\frac{1}{4}$ teaspoon garlic powder, and cook over low heat until the cheese is completely melted, 4 to 5 minutes. Pour the cheese mixture over the noodles and kale and stir to combine. Transfer the noodle-cheese mixture to the prepared baking dish. Sprinkle the topping evenly over the noodles and bake uncovered until heated through and bubbling, about 15 to 20 minutes.

· · · · · · · · ·

BLACK BEAN AND GREEN CHILE–STUFFED PEPPERS

Bell peppers overflow with black beans, tomatoes, green chiles, and noodles to make a hearty supper with a Tex-Mex accent. I like serving this with a green salad and perhaps a side of refried beans. Ro*Tel is the most popular brand of canned diced tomatoes with green chiles; if you can't find it, use a can of plain diced tomatoes and add a small (4-ounce) can drained green chiles. **Serves 4**

4 medium red or green bell peppers

salt

1 package ramen noodles, any flavor

2 teaspoons canola or vegetable oil

1 small onion, diced

1 (15-ounce) can black beans, drained and rinsed

1 (10-ounce) can diced tomatoes and green chiles (such as Ro*Tel brand)

2 tablespoons tomato paste

1 ½ teaspoons taco seasoning, plus more if desired

½ cup shredded Colby Jack or Monterey Jack cheese (2 ounces)

1. Preheat the oven to 350°F. Cut the tops off the bell peppers and remove the seeds and the white membranes. Sprinkle the insides of the bell peppers lightly with salt, place the peppers upright in a small baking or casserole dish, and roast until slightly softened, about 10 minutes. Remove from the oven and set aside.

2. While the bell peppers roast, break the cake of ramen noodles into several pieces and cook in boiling water for 3 minutes, or according to the package directions (discard the ramen seasoning). Drain and set aside.

3. Meanwhile, in a medium saucepan, heat the oil over medium-high heat. Add the onion and sauté until softened, about 5 minutes. Stir in the black beans, tomatoes with chiles, cooked ramen noodles, tomato paste, and taco seasoning. Cook over medium heat until the mixture begins to simmer, 7 to 10 minutes. Season to taste with salt or additional taco seasoning.

4. Fill the peppers with the ramen mixture and sprinkle cheese over the top. Bake until the cheese is melted and bubbly, about 20 minutes.

· · · · · · · ·

COOKING FOR COMPANY

When you're cooking for guests, it doesn't seem like ramen would be the type of meal that would impress them. But think again—with upscale ingredients and special techniques, even ramen can be part of a stellar meal. Challenge your culinary skills with these recipes that are sure to be a hit at your dinner table.

Make your mealtime more special, whether you're cooking for a significant other, hosting a dinner party, or just celebrating the end of the week. Here's how:

A tablecloth or place mats, and cloth napkins, can really dress up the table and add to a restaurant-quality experience. If you have good china, now's the time to get it out.

For a dinner party, serve an appetizer, even if it's something simple like dishes of nuts or olives, or a cheese plate. You can set out the appetizers in the living room so that your guests can relax and mingle while you're in the kitchen, putting last-minute touches on the meal.

Make a playlist or mix of your favorite music to play in the background. Well-chosen music puts everyone in a more relaxed mood and really adds to a festive atmosphere.

As you're cooking, clean as you go, and try to wash and put away all the dirty dishes, and wipe down the counters, just before your guests arrive. Most dinner parties eventually end up in the kitchen, so you'll want it looking decent. Plus, an empty sink and clean counters will make it easier to clear the table and clean up after your meal.

Don't forget the beverages! Search online for a fun, easy cocktail or sangria to make, choose a few bottles of wine, or make a batch of fresh lemonade or iced tea. Having a few choices on hand—with and without alcohol—will ensure that you can please everybody. Put a pitcher of ice water on the table, too.

SAUTÉED DUCK WITH SHALLOTS AND ARUGULA OVER HOISIN NOODLES

A juicy, rich duck breast is always an impressive main course for a dinner party. But don't be intimidated by this somewhat unusual meat: It's no more difficult to cook than a steak or a chicken breast. You might need to go to a specialty butcher or an ethnic grocery store to find duck, as many mainstream retailers don't carry it. When you cook the duck breast, save the fat—you can use it in place of cooking oil to add rich flavor to fried potatoes or other vegetables. **Serves 4**

4 duck breasts

salt and pepper

2 packages ramen noodles, any flavor

¼ cup hoisin sauce

4 shallots, peeled, halved, and thinly sliced

2 cups arugula

1. Rinse the duck breasts and pat dry with paper towels. Using a sharp knife, separate the breast halves if necessary, then score the breasts by cutting a few diagonal lines across the layer of fat, almost to the meat, in both directions, about ½ inch apart. Heat a large skillet over medium heat. Season the duck on both sides with salt and pepper. When the pan is very hot, add the duck, skin side down. Cook without disturbing until most of the fat has rendered and the exterior is crisp and browned, 7 to 10 minutes. Drain the excess fat, then turn the duck over and cook on the second side until the interior temperature reads 165°F on a meat thermometer, 4 to 5 minutes. Transfer the duck to a plate and cover loosely with aluminum foil to keep warm.

2. Meanwhile, cook the ramen noodles in boiling water for 3 minutes, or according to the package instructions (discard the ramen seasoning). Drain, return to the pot, and toss with the hoisin sauce. Cover the pot to keep warm.

3. Once the duck is cooked, add the shallots to the skillet and cook over medium heat until softened and browned, about 5 minutes. Add the arugula and cook over low heat, just until wilted, 2 to 3 minutes. Season to taste with salt and pepper.

4. To plate, thinly slice each duck breast diagonally. Divide the noodles among four plates. Top each serving with the shallot-arugula mixture and a duck breast, fanning the slices slightly.

• • • • • • • • •

THYME-CRUSTED PORK LOIN

This elegant roasted pork dish is seasoned with a spicy-sweet combination of Dijon mustard, maple syrup, and thyme. It's remarkably easy to make and looks so elegant when it's sliced and plated. Serve this on a bed of sautéed greens, perhaps with brown rice pilaf, or couscous with pine nuts and dried cranberries. **Serves 4**

2 tablespoons maple syrup

2 teaspoons Dijon mustard

1 package ramen noodles, any flavor

2 teaspoons dried thyme

1 (1-pound) boneless pork loin roast, trimmed of excess fat

salt and pepper

1. Preheat the oven to 375°F. In a small bowl, stir together the maple syrup and Dijon mustard. Break the ramen noodles into the bowl of a food processor and pulse to grind until they resemble rolled oats (discard the ramen seasoning). Transfer the ground noodles to a shallow dish and stir in the thyme.

2. Season the pork on all sides with salt and pepper. Using a basting brush, coat the pork loin with the maple-mustard mixture. Roll the pork in the ramen mixture, making sure to coat the sides completely with the dry noodles. Place the pork on a roasting rack in a roasting pan (or use an ovenproof cooling rack set on a rimmed baking sheet).

3. Roast the pork loin until the internal temperature is 140°F on a meat thermometer, 20 to 25 minutes. Let cool on the rack for 5 minutes, then transfer to a cutting board and cut into round slices before serving.

• • • • • • • • •

THAI NOODLE BOWL WITH BARBECUED PORK

This recipe is inspired by an unforgettable dish I had at a restaurant that specializes in Thai-style street food. Don't be daunted by the long list of ingredients. Chances are you have a lot of these on hand already if you've been cooking many recipes from this book, and you'll be rewarded by the complex flavors of the finished dish. Be sure to allow enough time to marinate the pork—it should sit for at least three hours, if not overnight. **Serves 4**

1 tablespoon hoisin sauce

1 tablespoon honey

1 tablespoon soy sauce

1 tablespoon rice cooking wine

1 teaspoon five-spice powder

2 teaspoons sesame oil

2 teaspoons fish sauce

1½ teaspoons minced or grated fresh ginger, divided

½ teaspoon Thai chili sauce

1 pound boneless pork loin or pork butt

1 clove garlic, minced

2 packages ramen noodles, chili flavor

1½ cups chopped Chinese greens (such as green mustard, *choy sum*, or Chinese broccoli), mustard greens, or arugula

¼ cup rice vinegar

1 teaspoon yellow mustard

Garnishes:

2 scallions, thinly sliced

2 tablespoons chopped peanuts

2 tablespoons chopped fresh cilantro

1. In a small saucepan, combine the hoisin sauce, honey, soy sauce, rice cooking wine, five-spice powder, 1 teaspoon sesame oil, fish sauce, ½ teaspoon ginger, and chili sauce. Heat to a simmer over medium heat, then reduce the heat to low and simmer for 5 minutes. Remove from the heat and let cool to room temperature.

2. Rub the pork with the garlic and brush generously with half of the barbecue sauce. Place the pork in a zip-top bag or on a plate covered with plastic wrap and refrigerate for 3 hours or overnight. Store the rest of the sauce in a small bowl, covered, in the refrigerator.

3. Preheat the oven to 375°F. Remove the pork from the refrigerator, transfer to a roasting rack in a roasting pan (or an ovenproof cooling rack set on a rimmed baking sheet), and brush with the remaining barbecue sauce. Roast until the pork's internal temperature is 140°F on a meat thermometer, 20 to 25 minutes. Remove from the oven and set aside.

4. To make the Thai noodles, cook the ramen noodles and the greens in boiling water for 3 minutes (reserve 1 packet ramen seasoning and discard the other). Drain in a colander. While the noodles and greens are cooking, in a large bowl, whisk together the rice vinegar, mustard, remaining 1 teaspoon sesame oil, remaining 1 teaspoon ginger, and the reserved ramen seasoning. Add the cooked noodles and greens to the dressing in the bowl and toss to combine.

5. To serve, thinly slice the pork diagonally. Divide the noodle mixture among four bowls. Top with the pork and garnish with the scallions, peanuts, and cilantro.

· · · · · · · · ·

TEMPURA SHRIMP IN MISO-SCALLION SOUP

Deep-frying is a bit of a production, but it's worth the effort for guests. Just be sure you're ready to serve the shrimp right when they come out of the hot oil—tempura is best when it's hot. **Serves 4**

1 tablespoon wakame (dried seaweed)

4 cups plus 4 tablespoons water, divided

2 scallions, thinly sliced

1 pound soft tofu, cut into small cubes

3 tablespoons white miso

2 packages ramen noodles, any flavor

dash of soy sauce

vegetable or canola oil, for deep-frying

1½ cups all-purpose flour, divided

½ cup rice flour

1 large egg

¾ cup cold seltzer water

8 uncooked tail-on shrimp, peeled and deveined, patted dry

1. In a small bowl, soak the wakame in 2 tablespoons water for 10 minutes. In a large saucepan, combine 4 cups water, the soaked wakame, and the scallions and tofu. Bring to a simmer over medium-high heat and cook for 5 minutes. While the broth simmers, in a small bowl, combine the miso with just enough water to make a thin paste, about 2 tablespoons, stirring until smooth. Remove the broth from the heat and stir in the miso. Set aside. Cook the ramen noodles in a pot of boiling water for 3 minutes, or according to the package directions (discard the ramen seasoning). Drain and set aside.

2. Pour oil into a large heavy-bottomed pot to a depth of 3 inches. Heat the oil over medium-high heat until the temperature is 350° to 375°F on a deep-frying thermometer, about 10 minutes. When the oil is ready, lower the heat to maintain the proper temperature.

3. While the oil is heating, in a bowl, combine ½ cup all-purpose flour and the rice flour. Using a fork, stir in the egg and gradually stir in the cold seltzer water until the mixture is about the consistency of thick pancake batter. Place the remaining 1 cup flour in a medium bowl. Line a rimmed baking sheet with paper towels and set it next to the stove.

4. When the oil is ready, dredge a shrimp in the flour, dusting off any excess, then, holding the shrimp by its tail, dip it into the batter, holding it for a moment over the bowl to let any excess batter drip off. Carefully drop the battered shrimp into the hot oil, and repeat with the remaining shrimp, adding only as many at one time as will fit in the pot without crowding. Fry for 3 minutes, turning the shrimp over with a slotted spoon halfway through cooking. Transfer the cooked shrimp to the prepared baking sheet. Repeat the battering and cooking process with the remaining shrimp if necessary.

5. To serve, stir the noodles into the miso broth. Ladle the soup into four bowls, then rest two tempura shrimp in each bowl, leaning the tail against the edge of the bowl.

· · · · · · · · ·

CREAMY DILLED PASTA WITH SMOKED SALMON AND PEAS

Elegant and rich, this recipe is quick to make, and it's easily doubled if you're serving more than two. Pair it with a spinach salad, a baguette, and a very cold glass of white wine. Use hot-smoked salmon, which results in a flaky texture, rather than cold-smoked salmon, like lox.

Serves 2

4 ounces (½ cup) cream cheese

¼ cup half-and-half

¼ cup vermouth or white wine

2 tablespoons grated Parmesan cheese, plus more for serving

⅛ teaspoon garlic powder

pinch of grated nutmeg

2 teaspoons finely chopped dill

salt and pepper

1 package ramen noodles, any flavor

½ cup frozen peas

4 ounces hot-smoked salmon, chopped

1. In a small saucepan over medium-low heat, whisk together the cream cheese, half-and-half, and white wine. Bring to a simmer and add the Parmesan cheese, garlic powder, and nutmeg. Simmer over low heat, stirring frequently with a whisk, until the Parmesan has melted and the mixture is smooth and creamy. Stir in the dill, season to taste with salt and pepper, and cover the pan to keep warm.

2. In a small pot of boiling water, cook the ramen noodles and peas for 3 minutes (discard the ramen seasoning). Drain into a colander and immediately add to the pan of sauce, along with the salmon. Stir to combine completely and serve immediately, garnished with more Parmesan cheese.

· · · · · · · ·

SALMON CROQUETTES WITH CREAMY CHILI SAUCE

Ground in the food processor, dry ramen makes a good stand-in for bread crumbs, and it retains a nice crunch wherever it's used. The chili flavor seasoning packet is used both in the croquette breading and to flavor the yogurt-based sauce. **Serves 4**

1 package ramen noodles, chili flavor

2 (6-ounce) cans salmon, drained

1 tablespoon all-purpose flour

2 tablespoons mayonnaise

1 large egg, lightly beaten

1 tablespoon chopped fresh cilantro

1 scallion, minced

2 tablespoons vegetable or canola oil

½ cup plain yogurt

1. Break the ramen noodles into the bowl of a food processor and pulse until they resemble fine bread crumbs (reserve the ramen seasoning). In a bowl, combine the salmon, flour, mayonnaise, egg, cilantro, scallion, and 3 tablespoons ground ramen. Using your hands, form the salmon mixture into 4 patties. Place the patties on a plate, cover them with plastic wrap, and refrigerate for 30 minutes to allow them to firm up.

2. Meanwhile, put the remaining ground ramen noodles in a shallow bowl or pie plate, sprinkle in about ½ teaspoon of the ramen seasoning, and stir to combine.

3. When the salmon patties are cold and firm, remove them from the refrigerator and dredge each patty in the seasoned ground ramen. In a large nonstick skillet, heat the oil over medium-high heat. When the oil is hot enough that it sizzles, add the croquettes and cook until browned, about 9 minutes on each side.

4. In a small bowl, stir together the yogurt with the remaining ramen seasoning. Serve the sauce with the croquettes.

• • • • • • • •

SOY GRILLED TOFU ON GINGERY NOODLES

You don't have to serve meat for an elegant dinner. Tofu, when it's cut into "steaks," marinated, and grilled, makes a fine main course.

Serves 2

2 tablespoons soy sauce

1 teaspoon sesame oil

1 (14-ounce) block extra-firm tofu, sliced in half lengthwise

1 package ramen noodles, any flavor

¼ cup seasoned rice vinegar

¼ teaspoon grated fresh ginger

2 tablespoons chopped cashews

1 tablespoon chopped fresh mint

1. Heat a grill pan, electric grill, or gas or charcoal grill on high heat. In a small bowl, stir together the soy sauce and sesame oil. Brush both sides of the tofu with the soy sauce mixture. Grill the tofu until grill marks appear, about 5 minutes. Turn over and grill for 5 minutes longer on the second side.

2. Meanwhile, cook the ramen noodles in boiling water for 3 minutes, or according to the package directions (discard the ramen seasoning). In a small bowl, combine the rice vinegar and ginger. Drain the noodles, return to the pot, and drizzle with the vinegar mixture. Toss to coat.

3. To serve, divide the noodles between two shallow bowls or plates. Place a tofu steak on each bed of noodles. Sprinkle with the cashews and mint.

• • • • • • • • •

SALMON AND BOK CHOY IN PARCHMENT

*Food cooked in parchment (or en papillote, as the French say) is always
a statement: A sealed parchment package is set before the diner, and
as the package is opened, a puff of fragrant steam gives a hint to the
delicious food waiting inside. You can also cook this meal in pieces of
aluminum foil. Foil is easier to work with since it holds its shape better
when you crimp it, but the presentation isn't as pretty.* **Serves 4**

1 package ramen noodles,
any flavor

2 tablespoons soy sauce

1 tablespoon fresh lime juice

1 teaspoon grated fresh ginger

½ teaspoon sesame oil

2 heads baby bok choy, leaves
separated

4 (4 to 6-ounce) salmon fillets

1. Preheat the oven to 400°F. Fold four 12-inch squares of
parchment paper in half (Figure 1)and cut one-half of a heart in
each (Figure 2). Set aside.

2. Cook the ramen noodles in boiling water for 3 minutes,
or according to the package directions (discard the ramen
seasoning). Drain and set aside. While the noodles are cooking,
whisk together the soy sauce, lime juice, ginger, and sesame oil
in a small bowl and set aside.

3. On one side of each piece of parchment, and leaving at least
a 1-inch border, layer the noodles, a few leaves of bok choy
(folding the leaves in half if needed), and a salmon fillet (Figure
3). Drizzle about 1 tablespoon sauce over each salmon fillet.
To seal the parchment, fold it over the filling, and, beginning

with the top of the heart, make little overlapping folds to crimp the parchment (Figure 4). When you get to the pointed end, tuck the folded edge of the parchment underneath the package (Figure 5). Place the four packages on a rimmed baking sheet and bake for 15 minutes.

4. To serve, place a closed parchment package (Figure 6) on each plate and allow guests to open it themselves to reveal their meal.

• • • • • • • •

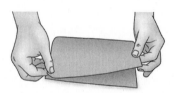

Figure 1

Figure 2

Figure 3

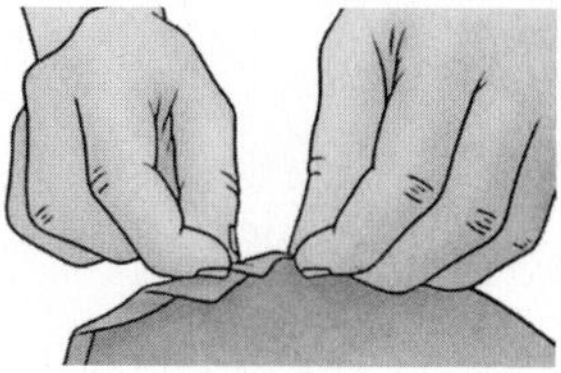

Figure 4

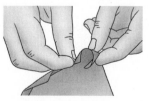

Figure 5

Figure 6

RAMEN NOODLES WITH WILD MUSHROOMS AND PARMESAN SAUCE

Indulge your dinner guests with an assortment of exotic mushrooms, sautéed and served atop pasta, dressed in a creamy Alfredo-type sauce. A gourmet food store will have the best selection of wild or exotic mushrooms; look for interesting varieties like maitake (also known as hen-of-the-woods, ram's head, and sheep's head), chanterelles, trumpet mushrooms, oyster mushrooms, or porcini. If you're trying to save money, you can combine the pricier, more exotic kinds with cremini mushrooms or strips of portobello mushrooms, which are less expensive.

Serves 4

1 tablespoon extra-virgin olive oil

6 ounces mixed wild mushrooms, stemmed where needed, and sliced

salt and pepper

2 tablespoons unsalted butter

2 tablespoons flour

1½ cups milk

½ cup grated Parmesan cheese, plus more for serving

⅛ teaspoon ground nutmeg

2 packages ramen noodles, any flavor

1. In a nonstick skillet, heat the olive oil over medium heat. Add the mushrooms and sauté until the mushrooms are soft and browned, 7 to 9 minutes. Season to taste with salt and pepper, and transfer to a bowl. Cover loosely with aluminum foil to keep warm.

2. In a small saucepan, melt the butter over medium-low heat. When the butter foams, whisk in the flour and continue whisking until the flour and butter form a thick paste. Gradually whisk in the milk, whisking between additions until the mixture is lump-free. When all of the milk has been added, bring it to a simmer and cook, stirring occasionally, until the sauce has thickened, about 5 minutes. Stir in the Parmesan cheese and the nutmeg and cook until the cheese has melted and the sauce is smooth and creamy, about 5 minutes.

3. Cook the ramen noodles in boiling water for 3 minutes, or according to the package directions (discard the ramen seasoning). Drain and return to the pot. Add the Parmesan sauce and stir to coat.

4. To serve, divide the noodles among four bowls. Top each bowl with a spoonful of mushrooms and a sprinkling of Parmesan cheese.

· · · · · · · · ·

TRUFFLED CHICKEN SALAD IN BIRD'S NESTS

An elegant appetizer for a dinner party, or an ideal light lunch, this chicken salad served in little noodle nests looks as impressive as it is delicious. Truffle oil is a bit pricey, but a little goes a long way, and it's so delicious I guarantee you'll find some fantastic uses for it: tossed with popcorn, drizzled over steamed vegetables like asparagus or green beans, or mixed into deviled egg filling, to name a few. To poach chicken for this recipe, see the instructions in the Chicken Potpie recipe (page 142). **Serves 4 as an entrée or 8 as an appetizer**

2 packages ramen noodles, chicken flavor

1 tablespoon extra-virgin olive oil

1 pound chopped cooked chicken meat

2 ribs celery, diced

1 shallot, finely chopped

1 cup quartered red grapes

½ cup chopped walnuts

2 tablespoons chopped fresh tarragon leaves, plus 8 sprigs tarragon, for garnish

¾ cup mayonnaise

2 tablespoons white wine vinegar

2 teaspoons truffle oil

salt and pepper

1. Preheat the oven to 350°F. Spray 8 cups of a standard muffin pan with cooking spray. Cook the ramen noodles in boiling water for 3 minutes, or according to the package directions (reserve the ramen seasoning). Drain, return to the pot, and toss with the olive oil and ½ teaspoon ramen seasoning (discard the remainder). When the noodles are cool enough to handle, press them against the bottom and sides of the muffin cups to form nests. Bake until the edges turn brown and the noodles begin to harden and turn crisp on the bottom and sides, 20 to 25 minutes. Remove from oven and let cool.

2. In a large bowl, combine the chicken, celery, shallot, grapes, walnuts, and tarragon. In a small bowl, combine the mayonnaise, vinegar, and 2 teaspoons truffle oil or to taste. Stir the mayonnaise mixture into the chicken mixture to coat. Season to taste with salt and pepper.

3. To serve, spoon a mound of the chicken salad into each bird's nest. Garnish each nest with a sprig of tarragon.

· · · · · · · · ·

FEEDING A CROWD

Next time you're agonizing over what appealing dish to serve at a party or tote to a potluck, just pull a couple packages of ramen noodles out of your pantry. You can't miss: Ramen is inexpensive, it cooks quickly, and it appeals to kids and adults alike. Plus, it's endlessly versatile—from a coconut-spiked fruit salad to a baked casserole to kabobs for the grill, you'll be set for your next shindig.

TURKEY NOODLE CASSEROLE

Hearty and filling, casseroles are the ideal way to feed a large group. This one is full of ingredients with mass appeal: ground turkey, black olives, corn, bacon, and cheese. Another good thing about casseroles? The leftovers are practically as good as the dish was the first time around. Feel free to substitute ingredients according to what you like or what you have on hand: The bacon can be omitted (just sauté the vegetables in a little oil), or you could use peas or mixed vegetables in place of the corn. You can also use ground beef instead of turkey.

Serves 8 to 10

5 slices bacon

2 medium onions, diced

2 ribs celery, diced

2 green bell peppers, diced

1 pound ground turkey

5 packages ramen noodles, any flavor, divided

1 (28-ounce) can diced tomatoes

1 (14-ounce) can sliced black olives, drained

1½ cups frozen corn, thawed

1 tablespoon ground cumin

salt and pepper

1¼ cups shredded cheddar cheese (5 ounces)

1. Preheat the oven to 375°F. Spray a 9 x 13-inch glass baking dish with cooking spray or lightly rub with oil, and line a plate with paper towels. Lay the bacon in a large nonstick pan. Heat over medium-high heat and cook, turning the bacon over halfway through cooking, until crisp, 7 to 9 minutes. Transfer to the paper towel–covered plate, and set aside. Pour out all but about 1 tablespoon bacon grease.

2. Add the onions, celery, and peppers to the pan and sauté over medium-high heat until the vegetables are softened, about 5 minutes. Add the ground turkey and cook until the turkey is browned and cooked through, 7 to 9 minutes.

3. Meanwhile, bring a large pot of water to a boil over high heat. Break 4 packages ramen noodles into 4 pieces each (discard the ramen seasoning). When the water is boiling, add the ramen noodles and boil for 2½ minutes. Drain and return to the pot. Add the tomatoes, olives, corn, and the turkey mixture, and stir well to combine. Season with the cumin, and salt and pepper to taste, and stir well.

4. Spread the mixture evenly in the prepared baking dish. In a medium bowl, crumble the remaining 1 package ramen noodles (discard the ramen seasoning) and add the cheese. Crumble the cooked bacon into the cheese mixture. Sprinkle the mixture evenly over the casserole. Bake until the cheese is melted, about 25 minutes.

· · · · · · · · ·

TUNA NOODLE CASSEROLE

This casserole is a riff on the traditional casseroles that call for a can of condensed cream of mushroom soup. Instead, fresh mushrooms and a roux (a mixture of melted butter and flour that is used to thicken a mixture) makes the creamy sauce. It's great on a cold winter night with a green salad and a loaf of bread. **Serves 8 to 10**

5 tablespoons unsalted butter, divided

1 large onion, chopped (about 1 cup)

8 ounces sliced cremini or white mushrooms

4 packages ramen noodles, chicken flavor, divided

2 teaspoons soy sauce

1 tablespoon red wine vinegar

4 tablespoons all-purpose flour

1 cup chicken broth

1¼ cups milk

1½ cups frozen peas

1 (12-ounce) can chunk light tuna packed in water, drained

1 tablespoon dried thyme

salt and pepper

¼ teaspoon hot sauce

1 cup shredded Colby or cheddar cheese (4 ounces)

1. Preheat the oven to 375°F. Spray a 9 x 13-inch glass baking dish with cooking spray or rub with butter. Bring a large pot of water to a boil over high heat.

2. In a large nonstick skillet, melt 1 tablespoon butter over medium-high heat. Add the onion and cook until softened, about 5 minutes. Add the mushrooms and cook until they release their liquid and the liquid evaporates, 5 to 7 minutes. Stir in 1 teaspoon ramen seasoning (discard the remainder), soy sauce, and red wine vinegar, and cook until most of the liquid has reduced, 1 to 2 minutes longer. Set aside.

3. In a medium saucepan, melt 3 tablespoons butter over medium heat. When the butter foams, whisk in the flour and continue whisking until the flour and butter form a thick paste, 1 to 2 minutes. Slowly whisk in the chicken broth and then the milk, whisking between additions until the mixture is smooth and lump-free. When all of the liquid has been added, bring to a simmer and cook until thickened, about 5 minutes, whisking frequently to make sure that the mixture doesn't stick to the bottom and scorch. With a wooden spoon, stir in the mushroom mixture, peas, tuna, and thyme.

4. Break 3 packages ramen noodles into 4 pieces each and cook them in the boiling water for 2½ minutes. Drain and return to the pot. Add the tuna mixture and stir to combine completely. Season to taste with salt and pepper. Add ¼ teaspoon hot sauce or to taste. Transfer the casserole mixture to the prepared baking dish.

5. Break the remaining 1 package ramen noodles into the bowl of a food processor and pulse until it resembles fine bread crumbs. Transfer to a bowl. Melt the remaining 1 tablespoon butter in the microwave and drizzle over the noodles. Stir in the cheese. Sprinkle the noodle mixture over the casserole. Bake until the cheese is melted, 20 to 30 minutes. Serve hot.

•••••••••

TERIYAKI-GLAZED KEBABS

Fire up the grill—these kebabs are the perfect thing to serve when you're expecting a yardful of hungry guests. You can make up the skewers in advance and keep them in the refrigerator until you're ready to go. The ingredients in this recipe are merely suggestions: Let your imagination and your taste buds guide you to create your own combinations. You can also set out the prepared chunks of meats and veggies in big bowls and invite your guests to assemble their own kebabs with their favorites. **Serves 8**

8 ounces white or cremini mushrooms, halved

1 pound shrimp, peeled and deveined

2 medium red or green bell peppers, cut into wide strips

2 medium zucchini, halved or quartered and cut into 1-inch chunks

1 (20-ounce) can pineapple chunks, drained

1 cup teriyaki sauce

4 packages ramen noodles, Oriental flavor

2 tablespoons sesame oil

1. Heat an outdoor grill to medium-high heat and oil the grate. If you're using wooden skewers, soak them in cold water for at least 30 minutes before grilling, so they don't burn. Using 16 skewers, thread an assortment of the mushrooms, shrimp, bell peppers, zucchini, and pineapple chunks onto each one, using 1 to 2 pieces of each food per skewer. Set skewers on a large tray or a rimmed baking sheet, and use a basting brush to coat them generously with teriyaki sauce.

2. Lay skewers across the grill and cook, turning over once or twice to evenly grill all sides, until the shrimp is opaque and the vegetables are slightly browned around the edges, about 4 to 6 minutes.

3. Meanwhile, cook the ramen noodles in boiling water for 3 minutes, or according to the package directions. Drain, return to the pot, drizzle with the sesame oil, and sprinkle with 1 teaspoon ramen seasoning (discard the remainder).

4. To serve, pull the cooked food off the skewers and serve on a bed of the noodles.

. . . .

SUMMER NOODLE SALAD WITH ZUCCHINI AND CARROTS

This salad can be thrown together in a matter of minutes, but it's particularly refreshing if you can chill it for a couple of hours before serving. Try adding chilled cooked edamame or strips of crunchy daikon for variety. **Serves 8**

juice of 3 limes

¼ cup soy sauce

1 tablespoon minced or grated fresh ginger

2 teaspoons honey

2 tablespoons vegetable or canola oil

4 packages ramen noodles, chili flavor

4 medium carrots, peeled and cut into matchsticks

2 medium zucchini, cut into matchsticks

2 scallions, thinly sliced diagonally

1 tablespoon sesame seeds

1. In a small bowl, whisk together the lime juice, soy sauce, ginger, honey, oil, and ½ teaspoon ramen seasoning (discard the remainder). Set aside.

2. Cook the ramen noodles in a large pot of boiling water for 3 minutes, or according to the package directions. Drain and rinse under cold water until the noodles are completely cooled. Place the noodles, carrots, zucchini, and scallions in a serving bowl and drizzle with the dressing. Toss to combine. Sprinkle with the sesame seeds.

· · · · · · · · ·

CRANBERRY-ORANGE POT ROAST

This sweet and savory pot roast is one of my friend Kelly's go-to meals when she has a bunch of guests to feed. It's made in a slow cooker, so you can do most of the work ahead of time, then just finish the dish and boil the noodles when your guests are ready to eat. **Serves 8**

4 packages ramen noodles, beef flavor

1 (14-ounce) can whole-berry cranberry sauce

grated zest and juice of 2 oranges (about 1 cup juice)

1 cup water

1 (1-inch) piece fresh ginger, peeled and quartered

5 cloves

1 cinnamon stick

3 tablespoons vegetable oil, divided

1 ½ large onions, chopped, divided

4 medium carrots, peeled and chopped

4 large cloves garlic, minced

¼ cup plus 1 tablespoon all-purpose flour, divided

1 teaspoon ground allspice

1 teaspoon ground nutmeg

3 pounds boneless rump roast

salt and pepper

1. Turn a slow cooker to low. Add 2 packets ramen seasoning (discard the remainder), cranberry sauce, orange zest and juice, water, ginger, cloves, and cinnamon stick, and stir to combine. Cover.

2. Heat 2 tablespoons of the oil in a large skillet over medium-high heat. Add about two-thirds of the onions and half of the carrots and cook, stirring occasionally, until the onions are translucent, about 5 minutes. Add the garlic and cook, stirring constantly, about 30 seconds. Add the vegetables to the slow cooker, stir to combine, and cover.

3. In a shallow bowl or pie plate, stir together ¼ cup flour, allspice, and nutmeg. Season the roast on all sides with salt and pepper. Dredge the roast in the flour mixture. Heat the skillet over medium-high heat, and add the roast. Brown on all sides, about 3 minutes per side. Add the roast to the slow cooker, cover, and cook for 6 hours on low.

4. Remove the roast from the slow cooker and set aside in a medium bowl. Strain the sauce, press out excess liquid, and discard the solids. Once the roast has cooled slightly, shred it into pieces with two forks. Set aside.

5. Heat 1 tablespoon oil in a large skillet over medium-high heat. Add the remaining onions and carrots and cook, stirring occasionally, until the onions are translucent. Add the remaining 1 tablespoon flour, and stir to coat the vegetables. Add 1 cup sauce from the slow cooker and stir to combine. Add the remaining sauce and bring to a simmer over medium-high heat. Cook until the sauce has reduced and begins to thicken, about 5 minutes. Add the shredded meat and cook until heated through, about 5 minutes.

6. Cook the ramen noodles in boiling water for 3 minutes, or according to the package directions. Drain the noodles. Divide the noodles among eight bowls and top each with shredded meat and sauce. Serve.

Variation:

If you don't have a slow cooker, you can make this dish in a Dutch oven or other heavy pot. Combine the ingredients in step 1 in a bowl, and use the Dutch oven on the stovetop to prepare step 2. After browning the meat, add the cranberry mixture to the Dutch oven and cook in a 200°F oven for about 4 hours, until the meat is fork-tender.

* * * * * * * *

RAMEN RED

My husband's family has a favorite dish they call Spaghetti Red. It's basically chili served on a bed of spaghetti noodles. I'm sure it was originally intended as a way for his mother to stretch out leftover chili so that it could make another meal for their family of six, but my husband likes the dish so much that he often asks for spaghetti noodles to go with his chili, even if we haven't reached the leftovers stage yet. Thus, Ramen Red was born. When you're making a big pot of chili to feed a passel of people, boiling up a few packages of ramen noodles is a way to make this dish more substantial, and for the chili to go a little further. Don't forget all the chili fixings: Shredded cheese, sour cream, chopped scallions, and black olives are my family's favorites. **Serves 8**

2 tablespoons vegetable or canola oil

2 medium onions, chopped

2 cloves garlic, minced

1 pound ground turkey or beef, or 1 (16-ounce) package frozen meatless crumbles, like MorningStar Farms

2 (28-ounce) cans crushed tomatoes

2 (16-ounce) cans kidney beans, drained and rinsed

1 (16-ounce) can black beans, drained and rinsed

1 (6-ounce) can tomato paste

1 tablespoon ground cumin

4 packages ramen noodles, chili flavor

1 teaspoon chili powder, medium heat, or more to taste

salt and pepper

Toppings:
shredded Colby cheese

chopped scallions

sliced black olives

sour cream

lime wedges

chopped fresh cilantro

1. Heat the oil in a large saucepan or Dutch oven over medium-high heat. Add the onions and sauté, stirring occasionally, until they're softened and translucent, about 5 minutes. Add the garlic and cook, stirring constantly, for 30 seconds.

2. Add the turkey or beef and cook, breaking up chunks with the spoon, until the meat is browned and cooked through, about 7 minutes. Use a spoon to remove any excess fat or liquid, then add the tomatoes, beans, and tomato paste, and stir to combine. Bring to a simmer and stir in the cumin, 1 packet ramen seasoning (discard the remainder), and chili powder. Season to taste with salt and pepper. Simmer until heated through and the flavors have had a chance to meld, 10 to 15 minutes.

3. Break the ramen noodles into large pieces and cook them in a large pot of boiling water for 3 minutes. Drain.

4. To serve, place the noodles in a shallow bowl and spoon the chili over the top. Allow guests to top their chili with the toppings of their choice.

• • • • • • • •

SPINACH AND SAUSAGE LASAGNE

Dry ramen noodles work just like no-bake lasagne noodles—you can layer the noodles dry in the pan, and while cooking, the sauce will soak in to soften the noodles. This version of lasagne is a fun alternative to the dish made with traditional noodles, and you can assemble it in a snap. I've used meatless sausage-style crumbles so that even vegetarians can enjoy this recipe (and meat eaters might never be the wiser), but if you prefer actual meat, just brown some ground sausage meat to use in its place. **Serves 8 to 10**

1 large egg

1 (15-ounce) container ricotta cheese

1 teaspoon dried Italian herbs or dried oregano

salt and pepper

1 (45-ounce) jar prepared tomato pasta sauce

6 packages ramen noodles, any flavor

2 cups shredded mozzarella cheese (8 ounces)

2 cups frozen spinach, thawed, excess water squeezed out

12 ounces sausage-style meatless crumbles, like MorningStar Farms

¼ cup Parmesan cheese

1. Preheat the oven to 375°F. In a medium bowl, lightly beat the egg with a fork, then stir in the ricotta cheese, herbs, and a pinch each of salt and pepper. Set aside.

2. Spread enough tomato sauce across the bottom of a 9 x 13-inch glass casserole dish to make a thin layer. Carefully break 3 cakes of ramen noodles in half where they're folded to make two thin layers from each. Arrange the six noodle layers in the bottom of the pan. Spread about half of the tomato sauce over the noodles. Spread the ricotta-egg mixture on top of the sauce. Next, layer about half of the cheese, all of the spinach, and half the meatless crumbles. Break the 3 remaining cakes of ramen into thin layers and arrange them in a single layer on top. Spread the rest of the tomato sauce over the noodles, then the rest of the meatless crumbles, and the rest of the cheese. Finish by sprinkling the lasagne with the Parmesan cheese.

3. Bake until the cheese is melted and the mixture is bubbly, 30 to 40 minutes. Serve hot or warm.

• • • • • • • •

TROPICAL FRUIT SALAD WITH CRISPY RAMEN-COCONUT TOPPING

This creamy, coconutty fruit salad is one of my mother's go-to recipes for summer parties or afternoon teas, although the crispy ramen and toasted coconut topping is my own twist. You can use any combination of fruit, but I love to include Mandarin oranges and canned pineapple. The oranges add a fancy touch, and the pineapple is such a nice tropical complement to the coconut. This salad will get watery and the ramen topping will get soggy if it sits too long before serving. If you're transporting it or you're not going to serve it right away, make and store the components (fruit, dressing, and topping) separately. Just before serving, drain any excess juice from the fruit mixture, stir the yogurt dressing into the salad, and sprinkle it with the ramen topping.

Serves 8 to 12

1 package ramen noodles, any flavor

1 tablespoon unsalted butter

1 tablespoon brown sugar

1 cup sweetened shredded coconut, divided

1 (20-ounce) can pineapple chunks, drained

1 (15-ounce) can Mandarin oranges, drained

1 cup grape halves

1 cup sliced strawberries (about half a pint or 6 ounces)

1½ cups cantaloupe chunks (from 1 cantaloupe)

6 ounces low-fat vanilla yogurt

½ teaspoon minced or grated fresh ginger

1. Line a rimmed baking sheet with parchment paper. In a small bowl, crush the ramen noodles with your hands into tiny pieces (discard the ramen seasoning). In a medium nonstick skillet over medium heat, melt the butter and brown sugar, stirring with a wooden spoon until the brown sugar is dissolved completely and the mixture is syrupy. Add the crushed ramen noodles and ½ cup coconut and cook, stirring constantly, until the coconut turns golden brown, 2 to 3 minutes. Watch the mixture carefully to keep the coconut from getting too dark or burning. Spread the ramen mixture on the prepared baking sheet to cool.

2. In a serving bowl, combine the pineapple, Mandarin oranges, grapes, strawberries, and cantaloupe. In a small bowl, stir together the yogurt, the remaining ½ cup coconut, and the ginger. Stir to combine. Stir the yogurt dressing into the fruit salad, mixing well to coat the fruit completely. Just before serving, sprinkle the salad with the crispy ramen topping. Serve immediately.

· · · · · · · · ·

RAMEN MARY

My friend Adam, who tended bar at a place I used to frequent in Brooklyn, makes the best Bloody Mary I've ever had. So when I had the idea that the unused seasoning packets from a package of ramen would nicely flavor a batch of Bloody Mary mix, I knew just the right person to ask about it. Adam rose to the occasion, developing a fantastic mix that is the perfect thing to serve at a brunch or the next time you have friends over to watch a big sports match. **Serves 8 to 10**

2 quarts tomato juice

4 ounces prepared horseradish (not cream style)

juice of 1½ lemons

juice of 2½ limes

2 tablespoons Worcestershire sauce

1 beef flavor ramen seasoning packet

2 teaspoons cracked black pepper

½ teaspoon salt or celery salt

1 teaspoon Tabasco sauce (chipotle Tabasco will add smokiness and depth)

Vodka

Garnishes:

lemon and lime wedges

celery sticks

pickled green beans

olives

large boiled shrimp

1. In a pitcher, stir together the tomato juice, horseradish, lemon juice, lime juice, Worcestershire sauce, and ramen seasoning. Add 2 teaspoons pepper, ½ teaspoon salt, and 1 teaspoon Tabasco sauce, or to taste. Refrigerate until needed.

2. To prepare a drink, fill a pint glass with ice, add 2 ounces vodka, and fill the rest of the glass with Bloody Mary mix. Shake to combine. Top with the garnish of your choice.

· · · · · · · ·

DESSERTS AND SWEETS

Ramen noodles as dessert? Sure! This assortment of treats uses ramen noodles in unconventional ways to add crunchy or chewy texture to a variety of cakes, cookies, candies, and more. You'll be surprised at how well ramen works in sweets.

CANDIED RAMEN SPRINKLE

This versatile topping adds sweet crunch to ice cream, yogurt, baked goods, and fruit salad. If you're making this on the stove, be sure to stir it often and watch it carefully—it can easily scorch. **Makes ¾ cup**

1 package ramen noodles, any flavor

1 tablespoon unsalted butter

2 tablespoons brown sugar

¼ teaspoon ground cinnamon

1. **Stovetop Directions:** Crumble the ramen noodles into a medium bowl (discard the ramen seasoning). In a medium nonstick skillet, melt the butter over medium heat. Add the brown sugar and cinnamon, and stir until the sugar melts and the mixture is syrupy. Add the ramen, stirring to coat it with the sugar mixture and cook, stirring frequently, until the ramen begins to brown and the sugar mixture looks dry, about 5 minutes. Spread the noodles on a plate and let cool. They will keep for 4 to 5 days at room temperature in a sealed container or zip-top bag.

2. **Oven Directions:** Preheat the oven to 350°F. Line a rimmed baking sheet with parchment paper. Crumble the ramen noodles into a medium bowl (discard the ramen seasoning). Melt the butter in the microwave. Drizzle the butter over the ramen, and stir to combine. Stir in the brown sugar and cinnamon. Spread the ramen on the prepared baking sheet and bake until the ramen begins to brown and the sugar mixture looks dry, 5 to 8 minutes, stirring once halfway through cooking.

• • • • • • • •

LEMON-GINGER CHEESECAKE WITH RAMEN CRUST

My mother makes the best cheesecake in the world. It's rich and creamy (rather than dry and crumbly like New York–style cheesecakes), with a tangy layer of sour cream on top that nicely complements the sweeter, denser layer of cream cheese custard. I was inspired by her two-layered cheesecake for this recipe, which is subtly flavored with fresh ginger. In place of the graham cracker–crumb crust that my mom makes, I've used crushed ramen. **Makes 8**

2 packages ramen noodles, any flavor

¼ cup brown sugar

1 teaspoon ground ginger

5 tablespoons unsalted butter, melted

1 pound cream cheese, softened

1 teaspoon vanilla extract

¾ cup granulated sugar, divided

2 large eggs

⅓ cup heavy cream

1 tablespoon grated fresh ginger

8 ounces sour cream

¼ cup lemon juice

fresh fruit or fruit preserves, to serve

1. Preheat the oven to 350°F. To make the crust, break the ramen noodles into the bowl of a food processor (discard the ramen seasoning) and pulse until they resemble fine bread crumbs. Add the brown sugar and ginger, and pulse to combine. Drizzle the melted butter over the noodle mixture and pulse a few times until it forms clumps. Press the mixture evenly into a 9-inch springform pan or a 9-inch deep-dish pie pan. If you're using a springform pan, the crust should come up along the sides just a little bit, but if you're using a pie pan, make sure the crust reaches the top of the pan. Bake until the crust is firm to the touch, 8 to 10 minutes. Cool for 10 minutes before filling.

2. To make the filling, beat the cream cheese in a stand mixer or in a large bowl with a handheld mixer until smooth. Add the vanilla and ½ cup sugar, and beat until smooth. Add the eggs one at a time, beating until they are well mixed. Beat in the heavy cream and ginger. Pour the filling into the cooled pie crust, scraping the bowl with a rubber spatula to get all the filling. Bake at 350°F until set, about 20 minutes. Remove from the oven, reduce the oven temperature to 300°F, and cool the cheesecake for 20 minutes.

3. While the cheesecake cools, stir together the sour cream, the remaining ¼ cup sugar, and the lemon juice. Spread the sour cream mixture over the cooled cheesecake and bake until set, about 5 minutes. Let cool on a rack for 30 to 40 minutes, then cover and chill for several hours or overnight in the refrigerator. The cheesecake is best eaten within a day or two, or the crust will get soggy. Top with fresh fruit, such as blueberries or peaches, or drizzle with blackberry, blueberry, or raspberry preserves.

• • • • • • • •

RAMEN-MALLOW CRISPY TREATS

Did you know those ubiquitous confections made with crisped rice cereal can be made with dry ramen noodles and produce just as delicious results? A package of ramen is just enough to make four squares, the perfect-size batch for just one or two people. If you don't have a baking dish small enough (4 or 5 inches square is ideal), you could use a plastic sandwich-size food-storage container, or just shape them free-form. **Makes 4 squares**

1 package ramen noodles, any flavor

1 tablespoon unsalted butter, plus more for preparing the pan

1½ cups mini marshmallows

pinch of salt

1. Butter a small (about 5 inches square) baking pan or heatproof plastic container. Crumble the ramen noodles into a medium bowl (discard the ramen seasoning). In a small saucepan, melt the butter over low heat. Add the marshmallows and melt, stirring frequently, until they are smooth and completely melted. Remove from the heat, add the crumbled ramen noodles and salt, and stir to coat the noodles completely with the marshmallow mixture. Press the mixture into the prepared container, making sure it is an even thickness. Allow to cool completely before cutting.

• • • • • • • •

CHOCOLATE PEANUT HAYSTACKS

Next time you're asked to bring a treat to a party or a meeting, whip up a batch or two of these haystack candies. They're easy to make and require only four ingredients, ones that you probably have in your cupboard already. **Makes 1 dozen haystacks**

½ cup semisweet chocolate chips

2 tablespoons smooth peanut butter

1 package ramen noodles, any flavor

½ cup roasted shelled peanuts

1. Line a rimmed baking sheet with parchment paper. In a double boiler or in the microwave, melt the chocolate chips, stirring until the chocolate is smooth. Stir in the peanut butter.

2. Crumble the ramen noodles into a medium bowl and add the peanuts (discard the ramen seasoning). Stir in the chocolate mixture, coating the ramen and nuts completely. Drop the mixture by the spoonful onto the prepared baking sheet. Refrigerate until firm, 1 to 2 hours, or overnight. Keep refrigerated or store in a cool place.

• • • • • • • • •

PINEAPPLE UPSIDE-DOWN CAKE WITH CANDIED NOODLES

Gooey, caramelly pineapple upside-down cake is so easy to make when you use a cake mix. And strewn in between the pineapple rings, cooked ramen noodles become almost candylike, with a deliciously chewy texture. The best cake mix for this recipe is one that has pudding in the mix, or that touts itself as moist. **Makes 1 (9 x 13-inch) cake; serves 8 to 10**

1 package ramen noodles, any flavor

1 (20-ounce) can pineapple rings

1 (18-ounce) package yellow cake mix

3 large eggs, or as instructed on the cake mix package

1/3 cup oil, or as instructed on the cake mix package

5 tablespoons unsalted butter

1 cup brown sugar

1 (14-ounce) jar maraschino cherries

coconut or vanilla-caramel ice cream, to serve

1. Preheat the oven to 350°F. Cook the ramen noodles in boiling water for 3 minutes, or according to the package directions (discard the ramen seasoning). Drain and set aside.

2. Strain the juice from the can of pineapple rings into a liquid measuring cup. Add enough water to make 1 cup or the amount of water needed in the cake mix instructions. Make the cake batter according to the package instructions, using the cake mix, eggs, and oil, and the pineapple juice instead of water.

3. Place the butter in a glass 9 x 13-inch baking dish, and put the dish in the oven as it preheats until the butter melts. Remove the dish from the oven and sprinkle the brown sugar evenly over the melted butter. Arrange the pineapple rings in two rows of four in the pan. Place a cherry in the center of each ring, and add more cherries around the pineapples. Spread some ramen noodles around any spaces in the pan that are uncovered by the pineapple. Spoon the cake batter over the fruit and noodles in the pan, spreading it with a spatula to make sure it is even.

4. Bake the cake until a toothpick inserted into the middle comes out dry, 45 to 55 minutes. Put a heatproof platter or baking sheet upside-down over the cake, turn the plate and the cake over, and leave the pan over the cake for a few minutes to let the caramel drizzle onto the cake before removing the pan. Store the cake covered loosely with plastic wrap for up to 2 to 3 days. Serve warm with scoops of ice cream.

· · · · · · · · ·

RAMEN NOODLE PUDDING

This recipe is inspired by my grandmother's noodle kugel, a Jewish dish that she served for the Jewish new year. Traditionally, kugel is made with wide egg noodles, but in this version the pudding is less dense and has a creamier consistency. **Serves 4 to 6**

3 large eggs

⅔ cup sugar

½ cup sour cream

½ cup applesauce

2 teaspoons ground cinnamon

½ teaspoon ground ginger

2 packages ramen noodles, any flavor

5 tablespoons unsalted butter, diced

½ cup raisins

1. Preheat the oven to 350°F. Butter a small (about 8 inches square) glass or metal baking dish. In a large bowl, whisk the eggs, then add the sugar, sour cream, applesauce, cinnamon, and ginger, and whisk to combine.

2. Cook the ramen noodles in boiling water for 2½ minutes (discard the ramen seasoning). Drain the noodles, return to the pot, and toss with the butter until the butter is completely melted. Add the noodle mixture to the egg mixture and stir to completely coat the noodles. Stir in the raisins.

3. Transfer the combined mixture to the prepared baking dish. Bake until the pudding is set and no longer jiggly, 45 minutes to 1 hour. Serve warm, at room temperature, or chilled. The noodle pudding will keep for 3 to 4 days covered in the refrigerator.

· · · · · · · · ·

RETRO FRUIT SALAD

A friend brought a version of this fruit salad to a brunch, and it was the hit of the party. Everyone wanted to know about the sweet, creamy sauce. Imagine our surprise when we learned that it was made from a mixture of pudding mix and the juice from one of the cans of fruit! I just love how this dish seems like something my grandma might've served at one of her bridge parties. **Serves 8**

1 (20-ounce) can pineapple chunks

1 (3.4-ounce) package instant vanilla pudding mix

1 (10-ounce) jar cherry halves, drained

1 (15-ounce) can Mandarin oranges, drained

1 cup red or green grape halves

1 package ramen noodles, any flavor

1. Strain the juice from the can of pineapple chunks into a large bowl. Stir in the pudding mix, blending well until the mixture begins to thicken. Stir in the pineapple chunks, cherry halves, Mandarin oranges, and grapes.

2. Break the cake of noodles into about 8 chunks and cook in boiling water for 3 minutes, or according to the package directions (discard the ramen seasoning). Drain and rinse under cold water until cool. Shake excess water off the noodles and stir them into the fruit salad. Chill, covered, for at least 1 hour before serving.

Variations:

- Try substituting other pudding flavors, such as lemon, coconut, or banana.

- Add ½ cup slivered almonds or shelled pistachios.

- Garnish with dried coconut.

- Add other kinds of canned or fresh fruit, such as peeled, cubed apples or pears; canned peaches cut into chunks; or fresh berries like blueberries, strawberries, or blackberries.

· · · · · · · · ·

BUTTERSCOTCH-CRANBERRY MOUNDS

This no-bake cookie is a fun one to take to a potluck or picnic where there are kids—they love the supersweet butterscotch flavor and the tangy, chewy bits of dried cranberries. **Makes 12 to 15 candies**

1 package ramen noodles, any flavor

½ cup mini marshmallows

⅓ cup dried cranberries

1 cup butterscotch chips

¼ cup sweetened condensed milk

coarse salt

1. Line a large plate or a rimmed baking sheet with parchment paper. Crumble the ramen noodles into a large bowl and add the marshmallows and cranberries (discard the ramen seasoning). Set aside.

2. In a double boiler or a metal bowl set over simmering water, begin melting the butterscotch chips, stirring frequently and adding the condensed milk 1 tablespoon at a time as the chips melt, about 10 minutes. Eventually they will become thick, smooth, and syrupy, like thick melted chocolate.

3. Immediately stir the melted butterscotch chips into the ramen mixture along with a generous pinch of coarse salt. Mix with a spoon and then with your hands to completely coat the ramen mixture with the butterscotch. Using your hands, roll the mixture into 1-inch balls and set them on the prepared plate or rimmed baking sheet. Allow to cool and harden in a cool room or in the refrigerator for at least 1 hour.

· · · · · · · · ·

BLUEBERRY-PEACH CRISP WITH RAMEN-OATMEAL TOPPING

Fruit crisps are one of the joys of summer, and this one combines two of my favorite fruits. In the fall, you can make this with an equal amount of apples or pears, and perhaps use dried cranberries or raisins in place of the blueberries. Or, if fresh peaches aren't in season, try using frozen; an added advantage is that you don't have to do the work of peeling, pitting, and slicing them. Use the optional sugar in the filling if your peaches seem a little tart. **Serves 6 to 8**

2 tablespoons unsalted butter, plus more for preparing the pan

1 package ramen noodles, any flavor

2 tablespoons brown sugar

½ teaspoon ground cinnamon

½ cup rolled oats

¼ cup apple juice

2 teaspoons cornstarch

2 tablespoons granulated sugar (optional)

2 pounds peaches, peeled and sliced (see page 216)

1 cup blueberries

1. Preheat the oven to 375°F. Butter an 11 x 7-inch glass baking dish. Crumble the ramen noodles into a medium bowl (discard the ramen seasoning). Melt the butter in a small nonstick skillet. Add the brown sugar and cinnamon, and stir to combine. When the mixture becomes syrupy, add the crumbled ramen noodles and oats and stir to combine. Sauté for 2 to 3 minutes longer, and set aside.

2. In a medium bowl, whisk together the apple juice and cornstarch. Taste the peaches and add sugar if needed. Add the peaches and the blueberries, and stir to combine. Spoon the fruit into the prepared baking pan. Sprinkle with the noodle mixture. Bake until the fruit is bubbling and the topping is browned, about 30 minutes.

· · · · · · · · ·

HOW TO PEEL AND PIT PEACHES

1. Heat a large pot of water to a boil. Cut an X in the base of each peach. Cook the peaches in the boiling water for 20 seconds. Remove and rinse with cool water.

2. When the peaches are cool enough to handle, peel the skins, beginning with the cut part and using a paring knife if necessary.

3. To pit and slice the peaches, cut the peach down the middle, around the pit. Separate the two halves of the peach by twisting them in opposite directions. Cut the peach into quarters and pull the edges away from the pit, then slice the sections into thinner slices, if desired.

COCONUT-LIME BARS

Lemon or lime bars are one of my favorite bakery treats, so I was excited when my friend Kelley dreamed up a version that had a crust made of coconut and crushed ramen. Sprinkled with more toasted coconut on top, these bars are the perfect balance of tangy and sweet.

Makes 16 bars

1 package ramen noodles, any flavor

½ cup plus 2 tablespoons all-purpose flour, divided

¾ cup confectioners' sugar, divided

1 cup sweetened shredded coconut, divided

2 tablespoons grated lime zest, divided

½ teaspoon salt

4 tablespoons unsalted butter, cut into small cubes

¼ cup ice water

4 large eggs

1⅓ cups granulated sugar

1 teaspoon baking powder

½ cup lime juice (from 4 to 5 limes)

1. Preheat the oven to 350°F. Butter a 9-inch square baking dish. Break the ramen noodles into the bowl of a food processor and pulse until they resemble fine bread crumbs (discard the ramen seasoning). Add the ½ cup flour, ½ cup confectioners' sugar, ½ cup shredded coconut, 1 tablespoon lime zest, and salt, and pulse about 10 times to combine. Add the butter to the bowl and pulse about 10 more times to combine. Add half of the water and pulse a few times to combine. Add the remaining water and pulse until the dough forms a large ball, about

10 pulses. Scrape the sides of the food processor to add the remaining dough to the ball.

3. Place the dough in the prepared baking dish. Use your hands to press the dough into the bottom and a ¼ inch up the sides of the baking dish. Bake until lightly golden, about 20 minutes.

4. While the dough is baking, beat the eggs in a large bowl. Add the granulated sugar, the remaining 2 tablespoons flour, baking powder, lime juice, and the remaining 1 tablespoon lime zest. Whisk until completely combined.

5. Remove the crust from the oven, and reduce the heat to 325°F. Whisk the egg mixture again to recombine and pour it over the dough. Bake the bars until the filling is set and looks dry on the top, about 25 minutes. Remove from the oven and let cool on a wire rack.

6. Spread the remaining ¼ cup coconut on a rimmed baking sheet and bake at 325°F until lightly toasted, about 10 minutes. Remove from the oven and let cool.

7. Using a fine mesh strainer, sift the remaining ¼ cup confectioners' sugar over the top of the lime bars to coat lightly. Sprinkle the top with the toasted coconut. Cool completely before cutting into squares.

· · · · · · · · ·

ALMOND-COCONUT MACAROONS

Chewy macaroons are a delicious treat, and the addition of dried ramen and almonds gives them a little bit of crunch. The almond extract adds a rich, upscale flavor. **Makes 24 macaroons**

1 package ramen noodles, any flavor

1 (14-ounce) package sweetened shredded coconut

1 cup sliced almonds

1 (14-ounce) can sweetened condensed milk

1 teaspoon almond extract

1 teaspoon kosher salt

2 egg whites

1. Preheat the oven to 325°F. Line a rimmed baking sheet with parchment paper.

2. Crumble the ramen noodles into a large bowl and add the coconut, almonds, sweetened condensed milk, almond extract, and salt (discard the ramen seasoning). Stir to combine.

3. In a stand mixer or in a medium bowl with a handheld mixer, beat the egg whites until they make firm peaks.

4. Fold the egg whites into the ramen-coconut mixture.

5. Use your hands to roll tablespoons of the mixture into balls. Drop onto the prepared baking sheet. Bake until they look dry and lightly golden, about 25 minutes. Remove from the oven, transfer the macaroons to a wire rack, and cool completely. Macaroons are best eaten the day they are made.

• • • • • • • •

APPENDIX

Ramen Manufacturers and Retailers

Ramen is so ubiquitous you're likely to find packages even at a gas station or a convenience store. But if you're looking for unusual flavors, want to experiment with different brands, or if you prefer to buy in bulk, here are some of the main manufacturers and online retailers of ramen noodles.

Dr. McDougall's

Santa Rosa, California

800-367-3844

www.rightfoods.com

The ramen cups from this health food brand are baked, rather than fried, and made with meatless flavorings appropriate for vegetarians. Look for vegetarian chicken, vegan miso, and other flavors in its ramen line. They'll be found in natural food stores or the health food aisle of the supermarket.

KOA Mart

Los Angeles, California
213-272-3480
www.koamart.com

This online Korean food retailer has a wide selection of hard-to-find imported ramen brands and flavors, including Shin Ramyun and Sapporo Ichiban Ramen. Here, you'll find unusual flavors like anchovy, spicy seafood, black bean paste, spicy kelp, and spicy cuttlefish.

Koyo

Providence, Rhode Island
888-534-0246
www.koyonaturalfoods.com

More expensive than most mainstream ramen brands, Koyo uses organic and higher-quality ingredients like heirloom wheat and sea salt and contains no MSG. The products are vegan and come in flavors like mushroom, seaweed, tofu, miso, Asian vegetable, and lemongrass ginger. Also, the dry noodles are baked, rather than flash-fried like most. Look for this brand in natural food stores.

Maruchan

Irvine, California

949-789-2300

www.maruchan.com

In addition to the traditional flavors of beef, chicken, Oriental, and shrimp, Maruchan's ramen flavors include lime chili, lime shrimp, creamy chicken, and roast chicken. The company's Instant Lunch soup cups also come in picante beef, and hot and spicy with shrimp and cheddar cheese. The company also makes ramen noodles and instant lunch soups that have 35 percent less sodium than traditional instant ramen. The noodles on their own are vegetarian, but one of the only vegetarian seasoning packets Maruchan manufactures is mushroom flavor, which is not widely distributed.

Nissin Foods

Gardena, California

323-321-6453

www.nissinfoods.com

Nissin's Top Ramen packaged instant noodles come in chicken, shrimp, Oriental, beef, picante beef, and chili, while its Cup Noodles can also be found in flavors like hearty chicken, creamy chicken, spicy chile chicken, and salsa picante chicken. Top Ramen's Oriental flavor is vegetarian.

Nongshim

Rancho Cucamonga, California

909-484-1888

www.nongshimusa.com

This Korean instant noodle company's version of instant ramen noodles is ramyun, and flavors include shin ramyun (which is so spicy it "makes a man cry," according to the company's website), kimchi ramyun, and seafood ramyun. It's sold at many warehouse stores.

RamenBox

Los Angeles, California

www.ramenbox.com

This online ramen retailer carries a wide selection of different ramen brands and flavors (mostly imported varieties), which online shoppers can choose to fill a customized case. Unusual varieties include Paldo green tea ramen, Indomie BBQ chicken ramen, Nongshim chapghetti ramen, and WuMu shiitake spinach ramen. The site includes detailed descriptions of each flavor and reader reviews.

Sources for Other Ingredients

Most of the ingredients in this book can be found in your local supermarket, especially if it has a well-stocked Asian foods section. You can also find many ingredients in an Asian grocery store if you have one nearby. But if you have trouble locally, try shopping online at these sites:

Amazon

www.amazon.com

Ramen by the case, sauces, and seasonings

Asian Food Grocer

www.asianfoodgrocer.com

Imported ramen, sauce, vinegar, and seasonings, including *nori furikake*

Asian Supermarket 365

www.asiansupermarket365.com

Oils, seasonings, sauces, imported Nissin ramen noodles, and canned meats and seafoods

Earthy Delights

www.earthy.com

Chile sauces, fancy soy sauces, spring roll wrappers, rice vinegars, coconut milk, and fresh and dried mushrooms

H Mart

www.hmart.com

The online version of an Asian supermarket with locations on the East Coast, and in Illinois, Texas, Georgia, and California; ramen noodles, sauces and seasonings, seaweed, *nori furikake*, and miso paste

Temple of Thai

www.templeofthai.com

Thai ingredients, including fresh produce, curries, chiles, spices, coconut milk, and Mama Noodles brand ramen noodles

Conversions

MEASURE	EQUIVALENT	METRIC
1 teaspoon	--	5 milliliters
1 tablespoon	3 teaspoons	14.8 milliliters
1 cup	16 tablespoons	236.8 milliliters
1 pint	2 cups	473.6 milliliters
1 quart	4 cups	947.2 milliliters
1 liter	4 cups + 3½ tablespoons	1000 milliliters
1 ounce (dry)	2 tablespoons	28.35 grams
1 pound	16 ounces	453.49 grams
2.21 pounds	35.3 ounces	1 kilogram
270°F / 350°F	--	132°C / 177°C

RECIPE INDEX

A

B

C

ABOUT THE AUTHOR

Jessica Harlan has written about food and cooking for nearly two decades. A graduate of the Institute of Culinary Education, she has developed recipes for well-known food brands, toured olive oil and pasta factories in Italy, reported on the newest food trends at industry trade shows across the country, judged food competitions, interviewed celebrity chefs, and catered swanky Manhattan cocktail parties.

She writes about cooking equipment for About.com and is the kitchen tools columnist for *Clean Eating* magazine. Her work has also appeared in the *Time Out New York Eating and Drinking* guide, *Mobil Travel Guide Atlanta*, *Town and Country*, *Pilates Style*, and *Consumers Digest*.

She lives in Atlanta, Georgia, with her husband and two daughters.